FOREWORD BY: REV. GEORGE A...

SPIRITUAL DIAGNOSIS

UNDERSTANDING THE MYSTERY BEHIND YOUR MISERY

SPIRITUAL WARFARE AND DELIVERANCE BOOK

KWAKU BOACHIE (BROTHER KAY)

Unless otherwise indicated, all scriptural quotations in this book are from the New King James Version of the Bible (NKJV)

Outskirts Press, Inc.
http://www.outskirtspress.com

ISBN: 978-1-4787-4531-0

Outskirts Press and the "OP" logo are trademarks belonging to Outskirts Press, Inc.

PRINTED IN THE UNITED STATES OF AMERICA

DEDICATION

To the Lord Jesus my Savior. Thank you for giving me the wisdom to write this book. All that I am and all that I shall become, I owe it to you.

To my wife Esther Boachie, my son Sony, my daughters Sonia and Sarah, my mother Ms. Esther Omane, and my brothers Prince and Cecil. May the Lord bless you all for your love and support.

To my senior Pastor, Rev. George Addae-Mintah and Mama Julia, and to all the sons and daughters of Agape Life Ministries Inc. God bless you all for your love and support.

My appreciation also goes to all the sons and daughters of Fresh Fire Prayer Ministry Inc. God bless you all for your love and support.

Contents

ACKNOWLEDGEMENTS

Thank you Jesus for giving me the opportunity to use my gift and talent to magnify your name.

Pastor George Addae-Mintah, thank for your great teachings and the freedom you have given me to express the gift of God in my life.

Special thanks to Mama Julia Addae-Mintah and Sister Emefa K. Gbedemah. God bless you all for your hard work and commitment to this book.

Thank you Joey Ofori for all your help, may God bless you.

FOREWARD

In Spiritual Diagnosis, Kwaku Boachie is calling on the Body of Christ to confront, deal with, and overcome real problems that many of us choose to just endure till we are called home to heaven. Even though the focus of this book is problems with Satanic roots, the author adopts a balanced approach by pointing out that some problems are good because they are trials from God to mature us, some are due to our own sins, and others are physical or natural. He also supports his positions with scriptures and real life examples.

The package of salvation won for us by the death of Jesus Christ on the cross includes victory over all these real life problems and the author confronts the reader with the message of salvation. This is very important lest the reader gets the impression that the problems covered in the book can be solved without the redemptive work of Jesus Christ on the cross. There are many who are going from meeting to meeting thinking some pastor or prophet can solve their problem without their giving their life to Christ and living for Him. On the other hand, the book makes it clear that after salvation, you must confront and deal with these problems AND overcome them because that is our heritage and right.

Every reader needs to pay a lot of attention to the Spiritual Tips, Strategic Prayer Points, and Prophetic Declarations at the end of the book. Even though they may not apply to you today, it is always better to be proactive in your walk with God and deal with problems before they become issues. You notice that Jesus did the forty days fast to start His ministry and not after He started having problems in the ministry. We should not wait until a terminal disease strikes us before we start praying against premature death. At Agape Life Ministries, we have a retreat we call the Encounter God Retreat where we spend a weekend in teaching and warfare prayer to deal with bondages in all areas of our life. Reading this book reminded me of the Encounter God Retreat experience. May you have an encounter with God as you read this book.

Rev. George Addae-Mintah, Senior Pastor

Agape Life Ministries, Inc

RECOMMENDATIONS

After reading Spiritual Diagnosis, I am convinced that it will be a great blessing to anyone who reads this wonderful book just as I have been blessed by the insights that are shared by the writer. The author discusses topics that are very relevant and practical to everyday issues that believers deal with.

Becoming a Christian is like enlisting in the army, you either prepare to fight or be prepared to lose. Once you enter the army and train to condition yourself for the task ahead, there is no turning back. You have to come to terms with the fact that there is an enemy out there who is out to get you and you need to fight him with a goal to win. Even when you or others fall, you have to get up and continue fighting.

As long as the enemy is out there (Rev. 12 :7-12), we have to take up our weapons (the Word of God and prayer) and fight. And the good news for the Christian is that, Jesus has already won the victory. So sitting and not taking any action to claim what belongs to us means we have surrendered our victory to the enemy (Satan, our adversary goes to and fro seeking whom he may devour).

The book puts every issue that happens to the believer in the right perspective being physical or natural, and spiritual - exposing the work of the devil, which we sometimes mistake for natural causes. The book does not end there, but goes on to offer positive recommendations on how to handle each problem.

I do not only applaud the effort that was committed to writing this book, but I will highly recommend it as an appropriate tool for a Victorious Christian Lifestyle, Amen!

Mrs. Julia Addae-Mintah

Agape Life Ministries

HOW TO USE THIS BOOK

I am a firm believer that nothing in life happens by chance. I do believe that the message contained in this book can revolutionize your life if you let it. Please keep in mind that this book is a manual of arms for Christian soldiers. It is not a devotional reader for the believer who is a part-time Christian. It is a deadly and a serious book for every dedicated Christian who is on the battlefield and wants to know how to win. It is not for believers who are jokers on the battlefront. Please don't speed-read these pages. Read them carefully and meditate on the scriptures. Spend time praying with the prayer topics given in this book. Ask the Holy Ghost to help you understand and assimilate the truths in this book. The truths in these pages will not do you any good if you don't put them into practice. Please don't put it on your bookshelf to collect dust.

Satan will no doubt do everything he can to keep you from benefiting from this book. He will make you doubt and perhaps make you critical as you read this book. He will arrange interruptions and distractions to detour you. I suggest you ask the Lord for help and protection as you study these pages. **"Greater is He who is in you than he who is in the world." (1 John 4:4)** You are positioned in Christ Jesus and delivered from the power of Satan. **You are seated in heavenly places far above principalities and powers because of Christ Jesus.**

Remember: you are not fighting for victory, but you are rather fighting from victory because Jesus Christ has already defeated Satan! I pray God's blessing for you as you read this book.

INTRODUCTION

Spiritual diagnosis is the ability to determine or analyze a problem, not with the intellect, but with discernment of the Holy Spirit. Spiritual diagnosis will help you to know what problems are the will of the Lord and those from the pit of hell. There are some problems, which can never be solved by manpower; they can only be solved by spiritual principles. And until we discover the root cause of the problem with the help of the Holy Spirit and spiritually deal with the problem, we will be wasting our time. In the physical world, when our car breaks down we take it to the mechanic shop to get it fixed. The first thing the mechanic will do before he does anything to your car is to diagnose your car to find out what is wrong with the car. Diagnosis helps the mechanic to find the specific problem with your car and after knowing the problem he/she begins to fix it. So it is with your body. When you are sick and you go to the hospital, the doctor will first diagnose you to find out what is actually wrong with your body before he/she prescribes medication for you. **It is the same in the spiritual realms. We have to allow the Holy Spirit to help us diagnose our problems so we can put physical problems and spiritual problems in their right perspectives.**

A few weeks ago, I had the privilege of attending a ten days prophetic crusade. It was at the end of the crusade that I became so convinced in my spirit that most of the problems we face in life have a spiritual connection and the remaining are due to natural causes. The Bible says, **"For we wrestle not against flesh and blood, but against** principalities, against powers, against the rulers of the darkness of this world, against spiritual wickedness in high places." (Ephesians 6:12)

I came to this conclusion due to the fact that most of the physical problems presented at the crusade by both believers and unbelievers such as barrenness, singleness, divorce, cancer, kidney stone, liver damage, heart attack, HIV, depression, fear, anxiety, untimely death, unexplainable setbacks in life, and financial crisis just to mention a few were diagnosed by the Holy Spirit to have spiritual root cause. The Bible says, **"For the weapons of our warfare are not carnal but mighty in God, for pulling down strongholds, casting down arguments and every high thing that exalted itself against the knowledge of God, bringing every thought into captivity to the obedience of Christ." (2 Corinthians 10:4 - 5)**

It is rather unfortunate that our education or so-called knowledge is blinding us from the works of the enemy. Today, modern Christian will interpret every problem or issue in their life by worldly measures. We believe that by exercising, dieting, and eating vegetables instead of fries, "fufu with light soup" (local Ghanaian dish) we will escape heart-related problems such as hypertension, heart attack, and live longer. This is partly true but not the whole truth, because some of the illnesses referred to by science as genetic are actually Satanic.

It is important to note that X-rays, CT scan, and MRI cannot detect demonic sicknesses. It takes the Holy Ghost to detect demonic implantations in our bodies. There is no amount of counseling sessions with a psychologist that can solve a marriage that is falling apart, which has its root cause from an agent of the devil. Until that agent sponsored by the devil is cast out or the witchcraft activity influencing the marriage is stopped by fervent prayers, that marriage is bound to fail. The Bible declares, **"The kingdom of heaven is like a man who sowed good seed in his field; but while men slept, his enemy came and sowed tares among the wheat and went away. So the servants of the owner came and said to him, 'sir, did you not sow good seed in**

the field? How then does it have tares?' He said to them, 'An enemy has done this." (Matthew 13: 24-28)

Note here that the sower (God) sowed a good seed, which represents a good marriage, job, health, peace, joy, love, and a fruitful life; however, when men slept which also represents spiritual dullness, spiritual insensitivity, and spiritual deadness the enemy (Satan) came to sow a bad seed; representing sickness, poverty, hate, discord, untimely death, setbacks, depression, anxiety, fear, and failures.

When Jesus found his disciples sleeping just before he was arrested for crucifixion, he told them to watch and pray lest they fall into temptation or fall into the traps of the enemy. **It is about time we awoke from our spiritual laziness and with fasting and fervent prayers destroy the works of the enemy**. Jesus has handed unto believers all authority in heaven and on the earth to destroy the works of the devil.

"I have given you authority to trample on snakes and scorpions and to overcome all the power of the enemy; nothing will harm you." (Luke 10:19)

Jesus has instructed us to heal the sick, cleanse the lepers, raise the dead, and cast out demons. (Matthews 10:8)

"And there was war in heaven, Michael and his angels fought against the dragon and the dragon fought and his angels. And prevailed not; neither was their place found anymore in heaven. "Therefore rejoice ye heavens, and ye that dwell in them. Woe to the inhabitants of the earth and of the sea! For the devil is come down unto you, having great wrath, because he knoweth that he hath but a short time."(Revelation 12:7 - 8)

The devil is doing his best to spend the short time very well. There is a fierce battle going on every day between two opposing forces. This battle is between light and darkness, good and evil, right and wrong, negative and positive powers. You may not believe it. But whether you believe it or not, you are involved in the battle anyway.

There is no neutral ground or demilitarized zone. Every Christian is a soldier and as a soldier of the Lord Jesus, you cannot say that you will not shoot anybody in a war or nobody should shoot you in warfare. **It is either you fight in the name of Jesus to become a victor or you just sit down and become a victim to the prowls of the enemy. It is that simple. It is either you sink or swim.**

Satan is a very clever strategist and a stubborn fighter. He refuses to acknowledge defeat until he is completely defeated. This is the reason why all lost grounds must be recovered from him because he sometimes renews his attacks. **Any lost grounds you have recovered from him must be properly defended because it is not enough to possess your promised land, you must also defend it. Satan never gives up, he keeps trying. If he fails today he will try tomorrow. The devils' expulsion from heaven did not stop him. He did not give up.**

When Jesus was born as a fragile little baby, the devil tried to use King Herod to destroy Him. The devil failed because an angel of the Lord came to Joseph in the middle of the night and told Joseph and Mary to flee with the child to Egypt for safety. But the enemy didn't give up. He attacked again when he found Jesus in the desert, weakened by forty days of fasting. The devil employed temptation as his weapon to defeat Jesus. However, one more time he was defeated and Jesus was victorious. But the enemy still did not give up. He changed his tactics and launched another attack on Jesus Christ. This time he entered the hearts and minds of the political and religious authorities at that time to condemn Jesus and destroy His ministry. The political and the religious authorities were successful in condemning Jesus to death. Then Satan thought he had achieved his ultimate goal. He thought that Jesus was finally defeated and there was no more hope for sinful man. However, on the third day, the cold tomb was opened and death gave way to life. Jesus defeated the power of death and hell.

Since that time the devil no longer has any legal power to destroy any child of God who knows their rights in Jesus. The devil and his cohorts have been finally and decisively defeated. Jesus has given His victory to any Christian who desires to believe in Him and live an over comer's life. It is high time a believer replied with ten blows when witches and demons give us a pinch. So they will learn not to pinch us again.

It is time we used the resurrection power of Jesus Christ to arrest every spiritual jailer holding us captive. It is time we stopped being jokers on the battlefront, wasting the precious resurrection power of Jesus inside of us. All we need to do is a little fasting, praying, Bible studies, holiness, and a little faith and we will drive the enemy out of our territory.

CHAPTER 1

Body, Soul, and Spirit

MAN IS A spirit, he has a soul and he lives in a body. The Bible says, **"Now may the God of peace Himself sanctify you completely; and may your whole SPIRIT, SOUL, and BODY be preserved blameless at the coming of Our Lord Jesus Christ." (1 Thessalonians 5:23).**

Man is a spirit because he is made in the image and likeness of God. (Gen. 1:26) Jesus said, **"God is spirit, and those who worship Him must worship in spirit and truth." (John 4:24)**

The Bible says, "For which cause we faint not; but though our **OUTWARD MAN (body)** perish, yet the **INWARD MAN (spirit)** is renewed day by day." The inward man, or the spirit, has a soul, but the inward man is not the soul. The soul is made up of the mind, will, and emotions. When we accept Jesus as our Lord and personal Savior, we become born again. The spirit man is immediately regenerated. We are translated from darkness to the light, from hell to heaven. However, the new birth is not a rebirth of the human body or the mind, but it is a rebirth of the human spirit. That is why you will have to present your body to God as a living sacrifice and renew your mind with the word of God. The Bible declares, **"I beseech you therefore, brethren by the mercies of God, that you present your bodies a living sacrifice, holy, acceptable to God, which is your reasonable service. And do not be conformed to this world, but be transformed by the**

renewing of your mind, that you may prove what is good and acceptable and perfect will of God." (Romans 12:1 - 2)

Note here that Paul wasn't talking to unbelievers but to the Roman
Christians. **"But as many as received Him, to them He gave the right
to become children of God, even to those who believe in His name."
(John 1:12)**

It is very possible for one to become a Christian today and still
have diabetes and hypertension in their body. The newly born again
believer may even struggle with lust of the eye, lust of the flesh, and
pride. **It takes the resurrection power of the Holy Spirit to gradu-
ally change the body and the soul.** This is the reason why the Bible
admonishes us to walk in the spirit and not satisfy the lustful desires
of the flesh. Paul said, **"But I keep my body, and bring it into subjec-
tion, lest, when I have preached to others, I myself should become
disqualified." (1 Corinthians 9:27).**

The body can become a slave to the demands and desires of the
soul if we walk in the flesh and not in the spirit. **For example, the
body can suffer from sexually transmitted diseases such as HIV after
the soul drives the body to lust after a prostitute. In the same vein
the soul can be enslaved or influenced by the activities of witchcraft,
voodoo, enchantment, and divination when we walk after the order
of the flesh.**

Judas Iscariot betrayed Jesus, because he allowed his soul to be
influenced by Satan. When his soul yielded to the Satanic advice to
betray his master Jesus, his body suffered destruction. The Bible declares, **"Men and brethren, this Scripture had to be fulfilled, which
the Holy Spirit spoke before by the mouth of David concerning
Judas, who became a guide to those who arrested Jesus; for he was
numbered with us and obtained a part in this ministry. Now this man
purchased a field with the wages of iniquity; and falling headlong,
he burst open in the middle and all his entrails gushed Out." (Acts
1:15-18)**

As believers we have to pray to our heavenly Father to have mercy on us and pour the Holy Spirit into us so that we don't walk after the flesh but walk after the order of the spirit. **Walking in the flesh can cause us big time.** Jonathan the son of King Saul was torn between **David (Spirit)** and his dad **Saul (flesh).** He sided with his father and went to battle with his dad king Saul and lost his dear life. The Bible declares, **"Walk in the Spirit, and ye shall not fulfill the lust of the flesh. For the sinful nature desires what is contrary to the Spirit, and the Spirit is contrary to the sinful nature. They are in conflict with each other, so that you do not do what you want. But if you are led by the Spirit, you are not under the law." (Galatians 5:16-18)**

"There is therefore now no condemnation to them which are in Christ Jesus, who walk not after the flesh, but after the spirit. For the law of the Spirit of life in Christ Jesus has made me free from the law of sin and death. For what the law could not do, in that it was weak through the flesh, God sending his own Son in the likeness of sinful flesh, and for sin, condemned sin in the flesh; that the righteousness of the law might be fulfilled in us, who walk not after the flesh, but after the Spirit. For they that are after the flesh do mind the things of the flesh; but they that are after the Spirit the things of the Spirit. For to be carnally minded is death; but to be spiritually minded is life and peace. Because the carnal mind is enmity against God: for it is not subject to the law of God, neither indeed can be. So then they that are in the flesh cannot please God. But you are not in the flesh, but in the Spirit, if so be that the Spirit of God dwell in you. Now if any man have not the Spirit of Christ he is none of His. And if Christ be in you, the body is dead because of sin; but the Spirit is life because of righteousness." (Romans 8:1-10)

CHAPTER 2

Problems and Diagnosis

AS LONG AS we live on this planet as human beings, we will have some problems. A problem is something that needs to be solved or something that we need to overcome. A problem is something that we don't want. A problem may be a mere challenge the believer has to overcome in order to possess his/her possession. The Bible says, **"And we know that God causes all things to work together for good for those who love God and are called according to His purpose for them." (Romans 8:28)**

God allows problems in the path of believers to test their faith so He can promote them. James said, **"Consider it all joy, my brethren, when you encounter various trials. Knowing that the testing of your faith produces endurance. And let endurance have its complete result. So that you may be perfect and complete, lacking nothing. Blessed is a man who perseveres under trial; for once he has been approved, he will receive the crown of life which the Lord has promised to who love Him." (James 1:2-4 and 12)**

"Be self-controlled and alert. Your enemy the devil prowls around like a roaring lion looking for someone to devour. Resist him, standing firm in the faith, because you know that your brothers throughout the world are undergoing the same kind of suffering. And the God of all grace, who called you to his eternal glory in Christ, after you have suffered a little while, will himself restore you and make you strong, firm and steadfast." (1 Peter 5:8 -10)

Sometimes, God has an interesting way of putting our blessing in the midst of problems. He then expects us to trust Him to help us overcome the problem to take possession of the blessing that is due us. We learn to give Him all the praise, glory, and thanks for what He has enabled us to accomplish. Our faith in Him is strengthened and we are humbled by how much we have accomplished through His grace and mercies. For example, God had promised the Israelites that they were going to inherit a land filled with milk and honey. As the Israelites were getting close to the Promised Land, Moses sent twelve spies to go and scout the place. So the people went to the Promised Land and came back with their report.

And they told him, and said, **"We came unto the land where you sent us, and surely it flowed with milk and honey; and this is the fruit of it. Nevertheless the people are strong that dwell in the land, and the cities are walled, and very great and moreover we saw the children of Anak there. The Amalekites dwell in the land of the South and the Hittites and the Jebusites, and the Amorites, dwell in the Mountains; and the Canaanites dwell by the sea and along the bank of the Jordan." (Numbers 13: 29)**

It was a fearful picture. The place was in a nutshell don't go area. It had been completely surrounded by enemies, and yet, it was the Promised Land God intended for His children. **As believers, some problems make us more sensitive and compassionate to the needs of other people. Problems are directed our way to make us wiser, stronger, and tougher for great blessings ahead of us. If we can only look at the bright side of every problem we face, we can learn from it and it will end up being a blessing to us.**

One day, Jesus Christ and His disciples saw a man who was blind from birth. And His disciples asked Him, saying, **"Teacher, who sinned, this man or his parents, that he was born blind?"** Jesus answered, "Neither this man nor his parents sinned, but that the works

of God should be revealed in him". (John 9:2 -3) God allowed the man to be blind so that He will show forth His miraculous power in his life. God sometimes allows the worse problems or situations to happen to us so that He may show us His glory.

How can there be a miracle if there is no obstacles, How can there be a comeback if there is no setbacks, How can you experience God's divine healing if you are not sick? How can you enjoy financial breakthrough if you are not broke or poor, and how can you get promotion or a better paying job if you don't lose the one you have now? Most of us pray to God to do a miracle in our lives; however when God begins the process of the miracles in our lives we start complaining. We want to maintain our comfort zone and get the miracles at the same time. It doesn't work that way. We can't eat our cake and have it at the same time. Something has to go for the new breakthrough to come to pass. In many cases the worse has to happen before the best shows up. So don't be afraid when you see your problem turn to be worse because God is about to perform a miracle and a wonder in the worst situation so that all will know that this is indeed the finger of the Almighty God in your life.

When Jesus heard that his friend Lazarus was sick, He said, **"this sickness is not unto death, but for the glory of God, that the Son of God may be glorified through it".** (John 11:4). The Bible says that Jesus delayed two more days when he heard that Lazarus was very sick and at the point of dying. The delay was meant to ensure that Lazarus was dead long enough that no one could misinterpret the miracle Jesus was about to perform on him as a fraud or mere resuscitation. When Jesus got to Bethany the town where Lazarus was dead, all were convinced that the man Lazarus was indeed dead and stinking badly. His situation was hopeless. It couldn't be changed and reversed.

Martha, the sister of Lazarus said to Jesus, **"Lord, if you had been here, my brother would not have died".** Jesus said to her, **"I am the resurrection and life. He who believes in Me, though he may die, he**

shall live. And whoever lives and believes in Me shall never die. Do you believe this?" Jesus is asking you right now that do you believe that the resurrection power of God can heal you from your sickness and that you shall not die but live and declare the wonderful works of the lord irrespective of what the doctors are saying.

Jesus said, **"Take away the stone".** Jesus is saying that you should take away the stone of unbelief and doubt. Martha, the sister of him who was dead, said to Him, **"Lord, by this time there is a stench, for he has been dead four days".** She is implying that the situation is impossible, hopeless, helpless, irreversible and unchangeable. **But the truth of the matter is that with God nothing is impossible. All things are possible with God and all things are possible to them that have faith and confidence in God.** Jesus said to her, **"Did I not say to you that if you believe you would see the glory of God?" (John 11:1- 44)**

My friend the spirit of God is speaking to you directly right now that if you believe God you will also see the glory of God in your problem. It doesn't matter how complicated, worse, and ugly the situation is if you will only believe you will see the glory of God manifested in your life. The resurrection power of God will bring any thing dead in your life back to life if you will only believe. Any dead dreams, visions, marriages, wombs, project, business, family, body organs can all come back to life by the resurrection power of Jesus Christ. **God is still in the business of bringing restoration to his children. The question here is do you believe?**

Isn't it so true that sometimes when you are facing problems the people around you especially your Christian brethren think you have sinned against the Lord that is the reason for the problem you are facing. Job's friends accused him falsely of sinning against the Lord because of the problems he was going through when indeed it was God who was rather boasting about the faithfulness of His servant Job to the devil. God allowed the devil to attack Job so He could bless Job even the more. **We have to learn to ignore the ignorant accusation of brethren during the times of difficulty.** God in due time will clear your name, vindicate you, bless, and promote you.

Look up to Jesus the author and finisher of your salvation during your difficult hour. He is the friend who sticks closer than a brother and He is a present help in time of trouble. He is with you all the way through the problem. He will strengthen you and help you to go through the problem and come out victoriously.

Some of us have to really thank God almighty for our problems. This is because if it hadn't been for problems, we will never have given our lives to God. God in His wisdom is using problems to draw some of us closer to Himself. **Some of us are so stubborn that God is using problems to humble and break us. If it hadn't been for problems, some of us will have no time for God. We are too busy with the cares of this present world that we have no time for God.** We practice part-time Christianity and our full-time is spent pursuing our own dreams. Today because of problems, we go to church services and all night prayer vigils with the quest of finding solutions from God to our problems and God is using the problem to make us learn to trust him. It is my prayer that our problems draw us closer to God and not drive us away from His presence. Apostle Paul said, **"Who shall separate us from the love of Christ? Shall tribulation, or distress, or persecution, or famine, or nakedness, or peril, or sword? As it is written, for your sake we are killed all day long; we are accounted as sheep for the slaughter. No, in all these we are more than conquerors through Him that loved us. For I am persuaded, that neither death, nor life, nor angels, nor principalities, nor powers, nor things present, nor things to come. Nor height, nor depth, nor any other creature, shall be able to separate us from the love of God, which is in Christ Jesus our Lord."(Romans 8:35-39)**

Whatever problems we face whether good, bad or ugly, God can turn it into our advantage. The scriptures says that anyone who put his trust in the Lord will never be put to shame and everyone who calls on the name of the Lord will be saved (Roman 10:11 - 13) I see God turning every situation you are going through to your favor. I see

God turning your sorrows into joy, your defeat into victory, your failures into success, and your setbacks into a comeback. God will put a new song in your mouth, joy into your heart, and a dance at your feet. **The people who used to laugh at you will now laugh with you, and those same people who said 'who are you' they will now bow their heads in shame and say to you 'how are you'.**

"Behold, I am the LORD, the God of all flesh; is anything too difficult for Me?" (Jeremiah 32:27)

"But now, this is what the LORD says He who created you, O Jacob, He who formed you, O Israel: "Fear not, for I have redeemed you; I have summoned you by name; you are mine. When you pass through the waters, I will be with you; and when you pass through the rivers, they will not sweep over you. When you walk through the fire, you will not be burned; the flame will not set you ablaze. For I am the LORD, Your God, the Holy One of Israel." (Isaiah 4:1- 3)

"Remember the things I have done in the past. For I alone am God! I am God, and there is none like Me. Only I can tell you the future before it even happens. Everything I plan will come to pass, for I do whatever I wish." (Isaiah 46:9- 10)

Whatever God has said concerning your life will surely come to pass. The only thing that can prolong or stop the promises of God from manifesting in your life is your unbelief and sin. But I see you having faith in God and fulfilling His promises concerning you in Jesus' name. You are more than a conqueror in Jesus' name because greater is He who lives in you than any problem from the world. God's grace is sufficient for you in times of your weakness. It is when you are weak that you are in fact really strong, because Jesus' strength is made perfect in your weakness.

"Let the weak say I am strong and let the poor say I am rich." **(Joel 3:10)**

Let the word of God grow inside you; water it every day in prayer and confess the word out aloud. Let the word of God become in you

an overcoming force. Let it prevail and win over your problems. At first the seed of God's words might seem so small, while the problem stands against you like Mount Everest. The problem will roar at you saying, "You shall never be married, you can't have a child, you will never get healed, you are a failure, you will die, it is all over with you, and you can't overcome." But as the seed of God's Word grows and grows in you, it becomes bigger and mightier than the mountainous problem. **By your faith in Jesus, you can command every mountainous problem in your life to be removed and you can bet they will remove**. I see you breaking through like a hot knife through butter. May the good Lord lighten your burden and renew your strength in Jesus' name.

It is very important for us to understand that some problems are fueled from the pit of hell. These problems have their source from the devil and his cohorts. These problems are directed by Satan to destroy or thwart the promises and blessings of God for our lives.

"The thief comes only to steal and kill and destroy; I came that they may have life, and have it abundantly." (John 10:10)

"Be sober, and be vigilant; because your adversary the devil, as a roaring lion, walks about, seeking whom he may devour." (1 Peter 5:8)

It is about time we stopped saying that every thing that comes our way is the will of the Lord. Sometimes God gives good things to us only for the devil to come and steal it from us when we are not mindful of his devices. It is high time we stopped being jokers on the battlefield. Resist the devil from your life and your family and he will flee from you.

The devil is always working around the clock and overtime seeking to cause pain and destruction to all believers and the work of Jesus. He is clever, ruthless, hostile, and aggressive in his incessant goal and ambition to steal, kill and destroy. Regardless of whether you realize it or not, Satan has targeted you as a victim. He is aware of your strengths, weaknesses, and he knows your address and telephone number. Somewhere in the shadows, he and his cohorts lurk, waiting, planning for the moment they will strike you and your family when you are caught off-guard.

After striking you, he desperately hopes you, like many Christians will remain ignorant of his reality so that you will blame his attack on God and somebody else. **He always seeks to divert attention and blame for his actions upon others.** But don't be fooled and make no mistake, he is the real enemy not your husband, wife, children, or your fellow brethren.

"For we do not wrestle against flesh and blood, but against principalities, against powers, against the rulers of the darkness of this age, against spiritual hosts of wickedness in the heavenly places." (Ephesians 6:12)

Satan is a liar and a deceiver, and he uses his deception as a weapon to gain advantage over those of us who are ignorant of the devices and the limitations of his power. Jesus has redeemed us from Satan's power and dominion over our lives by His death and His resurrection.

"Having disarmed principalities and powers, He made a public spectacle of them, triumphing over them in it." (Col. 2:15)

"...For this purpose the Son of God was manifested, that He might destroy the works of the devil." (1 John 3:8)

Every legal authority of Satan has been neutralized by the finished work of Jesus Christ on the cross. You have the right to use the authority of the name of Jesus to repel and drive Satan out of your territory and to break his grip over you and your family.

There are some problems, which I term as being mysterious. How can a Christian do all the right things and yet God allows something tragic to happen to him/her? Why do bad things happen to good people? I believe some of these questions can only be answered when we go to heaven to be with the Lord. Instead of asking why do bad thing happen to good people, it will be better to ask that when bad things happen to good people what do we do? I do understand that a lot of Christians believe that God owes them an apology for allowing bad things to happen to them, especially when He says He IS ALL POWERFUL GOD. **I will not even try to defend God but all I want you to know is that His thoughts are not our thoughts and His ways are not our ways. His wisdom far exceeds our little wisdom.**

You who are hurting because of the lost of a love one, you who feel disappointed in God because you believe He has abandoned you or forsaken you, I encourage you to renew your faith in God and keep on trusting Him even though it is very difficult because of all that you've been through. I believe God Himself will speak to you and bind your broken heart. One of the scriptures I find very difficult to understand and yet is the true word of God is **"in everything give thanks: for this is the will of God in Christ Jesus concerning you."(1 Thessalonians 5:18)**

We know very well that we need to be thankful to God when good things happen to us but how about the bad things? How do we thank God when our child is killed by drive by shooting? How do we thank God when we lose a loved one to cancer or car accident? How do we thank God when we lose our jobs and yet we have bills to pay? How do we thank God when almost seventy thousand people are killed due to the earthquake in Haiti? How can we simply be thankful in all things? How is it possible?

The Bible declares, **"consider what God has done: who can straighten what he has made crooked? When times are good, be happy; but when times are bad, consider: God has made the one as well as the other. Therefore, a man cannot discover anything about his future." (Ecclesiastes 7:10)**

The Bible talks about a very rich man called Job who lost all his goods, lost his family (sons and daughters), his home, and his health. His wife turned against him and his friends criticized him and yet this man of God had the **audacity of faith** to say blessed be the name of the Lord after losing everything he had in one day.

"The Lord gave, and the Lord has taken away; blessed be the name of the Lord."(Job 1:21)

"Shall we receive Good at the hand of God, and shall we not receive evil? "(JOB 2:10)

Job was fulfilling 1 Peter 4:16 **"yet, if any man suffer as a Christian, let him not be ashamed; but let him glorify God on this behalf"**.

The truth is that it is very hard to have a thankful and a grateful heart when things are bad. It is equally very hard to have a positive attitude when tragedy and hardships strike us. And yet God expects us to learn from Job and thank Him so we can get double reward for our trouble just like Job. I don't know what you are going through or what you've been through. May the good Lord give you peace in the midst of your storm. God is still in control. **I see God delivering you from the spirit of bitterness and anger in Jesus' name. May the Lord restore to you what you have lost. May the spirit of love and gratefulness fill your heart once again in Jesus' name. It is well with you in Jesus' name.**

There are some problems, which come as a result of our sins. Once we repent and make peace with God we will begin to have victory over that problem. **We have what is called personal spiritual chains or bondage. These problems are a direct result of gates and ladders we open or create for the devil to have easy assess into our lives.** For example, no amount of deliverance can save a person from a spiritual marriage if that individual continues to watch or keep pornographic materials. Once the gate is open to the devil and the ladder is in place, demons can come into the person at will to torment and frustrate that individual.

Demons cannot possess a believer but they can surely suppress and oppress the believer and make their lives miserable. We can only close Satanic gates and remove Satanic ladders if we genuinely repent from our sins and do away with those things which cause us to fall into the trap of the enemy. **Some of us opened the gates into our lives, when we sought help from a fetish priest, spiritual churches** where angels are worshipped, fortune tellers, joined freemason societies, committed adultery or fornication, read demonic books, magic, watched pornographic materials, drank holy water, joined occult groups, burned incense and candles to invite spirits, Yoga, and involved ourselves in some evil traditional practices, transcendental meditation and palm readings.

Many people are under silent bondage but they cannot talk to anybody about what they are going through. **Personal spiritual chains and covenants can be effectively broken by us renouncing (to give up by formal declaration, or put aside voluntarily) our association with the Satanic network in Jesus' name. We have to also revoke (to take back or withdraw; annul, cancel or reverse) any covenant we made with any secret society in Jesus' name. This is why it is important that we confess our sins to God every time we pray.** King Solomon wrote, **"He who covers his sins will not prosper, but whoever confesses and forsakes them will have mercy." (Proverbs 28:13)**

There is only one-way people can rid themselves of their sins. **They must repent, confess, and abandon them**. The love and the blood of Jesus Christ can cleanse us from all our sins. (Isaiah 1: 18).

"Come now, and let us reason together, Says the LORD, "Though your sins are like scarlet, They shall be white as snow; Though they are red like crimson, They shall be as wool." (Isaiah 1:18)

God sent Jonah to Nineveh, but Jonah decided to disobey God and he boarded a ship to go to Tarshish instead. So the Lord and not Satan decided to fight Jonah. God commanded the wind to rise against Jonah, and when they threw Jonah overboard, God again commanded the big fish to swallow him. When God is fighting you, the only solution is obedience. The Bible declares that an ailing man stood by the pool of Bethesda for 38 years without receiving any form of healing. He was in the position where Jesus was passing by. Jesus healed him and warned him not to sin any more, lest a terrible thing come upon him. It was at that point that the man realized that he had been sick for 38 years because of his sins. It was sin that had tied him down. If God felt that the only way to remove sins from the world was for His own Son to die, then we should know that sin is a serious problem. May the good Lord be merciful unto us and help us to overcome our sins. **"Submit to God. Resist the devil and he will flee from you." (James 4:7)**

Some of us Christians resist the devil but Satan does not flee from us. This is simply because we haven't submitted our whole life to God. Unfortunately, some believers also submit their whole life to God but they do not resist the devil so the devil still overcomes them with his attacks. We can only have total victory over Satan if we submit to God and resist the devil. It is then that the enemy will have no option but to flee from us because the **Spirit of the living God** will lift up a standard against him on our behalf.

Some of us believers will bear witness to the fact that our problems started when we surrendered our lives to God. When we were in the world of sin, we were at peace with our master, Satan. Satan knew that without Christ in our lives we were heading straight to eternal hell fire so he did not bother us. However, when we decided to leave the darkness of sin and enter into the marvelous light of Christ by accepting Jesus Christ as our Lord and personal Savior, then the battle with the devil began. Satan has decided to direct his rage at us because we are no more his.

There is what we call "rulers of the powers of darkness" who are willing to frustrate and destroy born again Christians. They use all sorts of methods to keep people from God. They can take advantage of your moral weakness and try to enslave you. Other times they can persecute you and even try to kill you for leaving their kingdom. **But the good new is that greater is Jesus, who is now in you that those demons, and no weapon formed against you shall ever prosper. When the demons come against you like a flood, the Spirit of God will form a wall of defense against them in Jesus' name. They shall try to fight against you but they will never prevail against you because God will be at your defense. Your God will be your shield,**

refuge, and strong fortress.

There are problems, which arise because we live in an imperfect world. The earth itself is cursed. If we fail to take good care of our body, we will get sick and even die. If you break the laws of nature you are sure to run into problems. If you jump from a tall story building, you can be sure that in no time you will be welcomed in heaven. This is because of law of gravity. If you break the law, it will break you. Try next time running through red light or speeding pass the speeding limit and you will soon learn the law of ticket. It takes common sense to overcome these problems not fasting and prayer. Well common sense is not common-to-common people so if you lack it you can still pray for it.

Please stop here and meditate on this song of encouragement. The Bible says David encouraged himself in the LORD.

He will do it again

May be you feel down and you think God has somehow forgotten you.
May be you are faced with circumstances you cannot get through.
Right now it seems there is no way and you are going under.
God has proven it time and again that He will fix it for you.

Chorus:
God will do it again
Just take a look at where you are now and where you've been.
Has He not always come through for you.
He is the same now as He was then.
You may not know how, you may not know when, but He will do it for you
He will do it again

God knows the pain you've been going through and how you are hurting.
He understands how your heart has been broken into.
He is the God of the sun, the stars and the sea.
He is your father.

He will calm your storm and He will find a way to fix your problem for you.

God will do it again for you.
He is still God, He will not fail you.
He is still God, He has not changed.
He is still God, He is fighting for you.
You may not know how, you may not know when but He will do it again.

Diagnosis is defined as the determination or analysis of the cause or nature of a problem or situation. It also means an answer or solution to a problematic situation. Spiritual can be defined as things pertaining to the spirit and soul. I will define spiritual as unseen reality. **Spiritual diagnosis is the ability to determine or analyze a problem not with the intellect but with discernment of the Holy Spirit. Spiritual diagnosis will help you to know what problems are the will of the Lord and those from the pit of hell. There are some problems, which can never be solved by manpower; they can only be solved by spiritual principles. And until we discover the root cause of the problem with the help of the Holy Spirit and spiritually deal with the problem, we will be wasting our time.** This is the main reason why God has blessed the body of Christ with spiritual gifts such as word of knowledge, gift of prophecy, and the discernment of spirit. The prophets are also vital in this area. They give us retrospective (past) knowledge and prospective (future) information to equip us. God also reveals the secret counsel of the enemy against us through our dreams. **Some covenants, yokes, and curses can only be broken, reversed, or revoked only when they are properly diagnosed spiritually. "And you shall know the truth and the truth shall set you free." (John 8: 32)**

There are some deep truths about our lives and the families we come from which can only be made known to us by the Holy Spirit. **It is time to discover to recover for to be rightly informed is to be transformed and to be uninformed is to be deformed.** Let us stop being jokers on the battlefront.

"Now concerning spiritual gifts, brethren, I do not want you to be ignorant."(1 Corinthians 12:1)

Discerning of Spirits

The gift of discerning of spirits is a supernatural gift given to the children of God to understand when God is working and when Satan is trying to deceive us. Remember that the devil always tries to appear as an angel of light. The gift of discerning of spirit will enable us to know who are a false prophet and a true prophet. It will also help us to better diagnose our daily problems to know which ones are the will of the Lord and those problems that come from Satan and his cohorts. The gift of discernment is a free gift from the Holy Spirit. If you ask God for it He will give it to you.

The Gift of Word of Knowledge

Word of knowledge is a supernatural gift from the Holy Ghost. The Holy Spirit can give you knowledge about the past, present, and the future of someone when you are praying for them. The Holy Spirit through the gift of word of knowledge can reveal to you the secret counsel of the enemy against your life, family and marriage so that you can pray against them. Let see how the word of knowledge works from this example.

"Now the king of Syria was making war against Israel; and he consulted with his servants, saying, "My camp will be in such and such a place." And the man of God (Elisha) sent to the king of Israel, saying, "Beware that you do not pass this place, for the Syrians are coming down there." Then the king of Israel sent someone to the place of which the man of God had told him. Thus he warned him, and he was watchful there, not just once or twice. Therefore the heart of the king of Syria was greatly troubled by this thing; and he called his servants and said to them, **"Will you not show me which of us is for the king of Israel?" And one of his servants said, "None, my lord, O king; but Elisha, the prophet who is in Israel, tells the king of Israel the words**

that you speak in your bedroom." (2 King 6:8 – 12)

The nation of Israel was saved many times from their enemies not by their army but by the word of knowledge from the prophet of God. Just imagine the number of mistakes and traps you and I could have avoided and escaped from if we operated in word of knowledge from the Holy Ghost. Most of us have become victims to the devil because we fell into his traps without us knowing it. **Marriages are being destroyed, families are been scattered and peoples health are failing all because we are not hearing from God to tell us the wick counsel of the enemy against us and our family. People are loosing huge sums of money in wrong investments, singles are marrying the wrong life partners, people have gotten themselves into business partnership with the wrong people which has cost them great pain and we are constantly making wrong decisions and choices because we cannot discern and have the proper word of knowledge for our lives. We are just falling into the traps of the enemy ignorantly.** Remember that only the Holy Spirit can reveal to you the secret counsel of the enemy against your life and your family. Word of knowledge is a free gift of the Holy Spirit and if you ask God, He will give it to you freely. Jesus received the revelation of Nathaniel under the fig tree and the condition of his heart through word of knowledge. (John 1:47-50).

The Gift of the Word of Wisdom

The gift of the word of wisdom goes hand in hand with word of knowledge. When God gives you the knowledge, the gift of the word of wisdom help you to properly apply the knowledge to get the best results. If you have knowledge and you don't have wisdom to apply the knowledge well you will still make mistakes or fall into the trap of the enemy. Wisdom is the correct application of knowledge. Let see how it works. In Genesis 41 vs. 14 to 16 says, **"Then Pharaoh sent and called Joseph, and they brought him quickly out of the dungeon; and he shaved, changed his clothing, and came to Pharaoh. And Pharaoh said to Joseph, "I have had a dream, and there is no one** who can interpret it. But I have heard it said of you that you can understand a dream, to interpret it". So Joseph answered Pharaoh, saying, "It is not in me; God will give Pharaoh an answer of peace".

After Joseph had given Pharaoh the interpretation or answer to his dream through word of knowledge, the gift of word of wisdom was in operation. HHe gave Pharaoh the wisest advice that made him next in power to Pharaoh. I tell you the truth when I say these gifts of the spirit are very powerful. We should all pray for them in our lives. It is enough of us praying to God for big cars, houses and money. Let us also spend time praying to get the gift of the spirit and our lives will never be the same. Let see how Joseph did it. **"And the dream was repeated to Pharaoh twice because the thing is established by God, and God will shortly bring it to pass. Now therefore, let Pharaoh select a discerning and wise man, and set him over the land of Egypt. Let Pharaoh do this, and let him appoint officers over the land, to collect one-fifth of the produce of the land of Egypt in the seven plentiful years. And let them gather all the food of those good years that are coming, and store up grain under the authority of Pharaoh, and let them keep food in the cities. Then that food shall be as a reserve for the land for the seven years of famine which shall be in the land of Egypt that the land may not perish during the famine."** (Genesis 41:32)

So the advice was good in the eyes of Pharaoh and in the eyes of all his servants. And Pharaoh said to his servants, **"Can we find such a one as this, a man in whom is the Spirit of God?" Then Pharaoh said to Joseph, "Inasmuch as God has shown you all this, there is no one as discerning and wise as you. You shall be over my house, and all my people shall be ruled according to your word; only in regard to the throne will I be greater than you." And Pharaoh said to Joseph, "See, I have set you over all the land of Egypt."** God used the gift of the Spirit to bring to pass his promise to Joseph. The Bible says that a man's gift will make a way for him. I encourage you to desire the gifts of the spirit and God will grant it to you to help you better diagnose your problems.

CHAPTER 3

Chief Complaint

MOST OF US have a catalog full of problems but the chief complaint is the major problem you are currently facing. At each stage in our lives, we will be presented with a major problem or challenge that outweighs all the other problems we have. This problem is number one on our prayer list. It compels us to pray to God for a solution, run after our pastors for help, and go from one crusade to another searching for solutions.

Hannah was driven to the temple of God to pray to Jehovah God for help because of her inability to give birth (Barrenness). Her chief complaint was barrenness. Abraham, the friend of God was very rich and highly blessed of God, but his chief complaint was that he had no son to inherit his blessing. A woman risked her life to touch Jesus with a touch of faith because her chief complaint was the problem with the issue of blood. Your chief complaints may be unemployment, barrenness, sickness, run-away husband or wife, a prodigal child, or a major setback in life. May be you are at the end of the road now and a particular problem seems to have caged you in, call on the Lord Jesus, and He will answer you. Whatever major complaint or problem you have, God is more than able to help you solve it.

Many believers narrate their chief complaint to everybody including the Gossipers National Congress (GNC) except the only one who should really know their problems, that is Jesus. Only God can truly help us or send people our way to help us. If God cannot help you then no man can help you. The Bible says, **"Never worry about anything. Instead, in every situation let your petitions be made known to God through prayers and requests, with thanksgiving. Then God's peace, which goes far beyond anything we can imagine, will guard your hearts and mind in union with the Messiah Jesus."** (Philippians 4:6 - 7)

CHAPTER 4

History of Problem

HISTORY OF PROBLEM deals with the root cause of our problems and how long we have been coping with the problems. The woman with the issue of blood had her problem with bleeding for twelve years. Jesus once healed a man at the pool of Bethesda who was lame for thirty-eight years. Abraham had his son Isaac when he was almost a hundred years old, and Sarah his wife ninety years. Jabez lived a life of pain from his childhood until his adulthood. Jabez prayed to the Lord God of Israel and his painful life experience was terminated (1 Chronicles 4:9-10).

There are some problems if we do not take care, we will take them to our graves. We can only defeat them by calling on the name of the Lord for help. It will interest you to know that Goliath had threatened the Israelites eighty-one times before David arrived at the battlefield. Perhaps your own physical or spiritual Goliath has also been threatening you for a long time. It is about time you arise and slay it in Jesus' name. If you stand and fight your Goliath, the problem in your family, marriage, and business will disappear completely in Jesus' name.

"Then should not this woman, a daughter of Abraham, whom Satan has kept bound for eighteen long years, be set free on the Sabbath day from what bound her?" (Luke 13:16)

Jesus commanded the spirit of infirmity to leave her and then the woman straighten up again. This daughter of Abraham had her problem for eighteen bad years. **The good news is that anyone who calls on the name of the Lord will be saved irrespective of how long you have had your problem.** I see God reversing the irreversible and doing the impossible in your life. Jesus said, **"With man this is impossible, but with God all things are possible."** (Matthew 19:26)

"If you can believe, all things are possible to him that Believes." (Mathew 17:20)

It doesn't matter your age God can still bless you with a child and a life's partner. Only believe and you shall see the glory of God in your life. I see God stepping into your situation and blowing your mind with surprises. You shall breakthrough, break forth, and break forward. I see God lifting limitation from you and breaking the yokes of your neck. It shall be well with you, so weep no more for help is on the way.

Everybody comes from a family and every family has its history. It is important that you know the history of your family especially if you are dealing with a strange problem in your life. Talk to your parents, grandparents, or family relations and find out more about your bloodline. It will amaze you what you might learn from the information you gather. **History helps us to know where we are coming from, where we are and where we ought to be.** History helps us avoid the mistakes of the past and make us wiser to confront the challenges of the future. **You need to know your family history.** Examples of the history of family related problems: (These are deep spiritual truths which can cause you to become uncomfortable but they are true.) **"He reveals deep and secret things; He knows what is in the darkness, and light dwells with Him."** (Daniel 2:22)

Names

Names are synonymous with our nature, and they are the legacies we leave for our children to inherit. The names we inherit can impart favor and blessing to us or we can inherit generational curses from the families we come from. A man's character is synonymous with his name, like a key it can open or close doors of opportunity depending on the inherent character and status of the bearer of the name. Names do not only identify a person but they also carry the character traits (behavior) of the bearer.

"Please, let not my Lord regard this scoundrel Nabal. For as his name is, so is he: Nabal is his name, and folly is with him!" (1 Samuel 25:25)

Without any controversy, the decisions and the choices of our ancestors can affect our now, future, and destiny. King Davids' wrong choice of sleeping with Bathsheba brought a curse onto his family. Nathan said to David **"You have killed Uriah the Hittite with the sword; you have taken his wife to be your wife, and have killed him with the sword of the people of Ammon. Now therefore, *the sword shall never depart from your house* because you have despised Me, and have taken the wife of Uriah the Hittite to be your wife." (2 Samuel 1:9)**

It was not long after Nathan's prophesy that the curse began to have its effect on David's family. David's first son Absalom murdered his own half brother Ammon.

"Now Absalom had commanded his servants, saying,

"Watch now, when Ammon's heart is merry with wine, and when I say to you, 'Strike Ammon' then kill him." (2 Samuel 13:28)

Jonathan, Ish-Bosheth, and Mephibosheth, son and grandsons of King Saul lost the kingship to the throne to David because of their father king Saul's disobedience to God. Some of us bear names of an ancestor who made very wrong choices in life because they did not know Jesus. Some of our ancestor's murdered innocent people in order to attained certain positions or thrones in the clan. These ignorant actions by our forefathers brought curses upon them and their descendants. Today after many decades if you happen to bear the name of that great ancestor, the devil can enforce the curse upon you and your family.

"And the passed by before him, and proclaimed, The Lord, The Lord God, merciful and gracious, longsuffering, and abundant in goodness and truth, keeping mercy for thousands, forgiving iniquity and transgression and sin, and that will by no means clear the guilty; visiting the iniquity of the fathers upon the children, and upon the children's children, unto the third and to the fourth generation." (Exodus 34:6-7)

The good news is that you can use the blood of Jesus to sanctify your name from every Satanic association from the past. Every yoke or curse attached to your name can be broken by the power of the Holy Spirit. **In your prayers, use the blood of Jesus to disconnect yourself from the sins of your ancestors and reconnect your body, soul, and spirit to Jesus so that the blessing of Abraham will begin to run through your family.** Jabez prayed to the Lord God and his name, which meant pain, was sanctified. God answered the prayers of Jabez and blessed his name and he became more honorable than all his brethren.

I see Jehovah God changing your name from Sarai (quarrelsome) to Sarah (princess; princess of the multitude), From Abram (Exalted Father) to Abraham (Father of a great multitude), from Jacob (Supplanter or deceiver) to Israel (prince or he who prevails with God). From now on may your name be sanctified, favored, and blessed of God. **Now that you are a believer, be mindful whom you name your children after so that they do not have to fight unnecessary battles in the future. Please do a background check of the person your children are named after.**

Marriage

Some marriages collapse due to Satanic manipulations. The devil may send a family relative, a friend or an agent to come and separate married couples. An enchantment or a spell from witchcraft spirits can cause a married man to abandon his wife and children for another woman. Dispute, quarrel, misunderstanding over a small issue can be sent from the pit of hell to bring about divorce. Sometimes the face of a wife can be altered so much that whenever the husband sees his wife, he automatically becomes angry without cause. There was one instance where the face of a married woman was spiritually turned into a goat. The woman did everything in the natural to please the husband but the more she became nice to the husband, the more the husband hated her. The problem was solved when one day the husband went for a prayer meeting and the spell was broken from his eyes. When he went home on that day he was surprised to see how beautiful and nice his wife actually was.

Please let us stop playing the devils blame games and start dealing with the root cause of the problem. Your wife is not the enemy; your husband is not the enemy, the archenemy is the devil. It is about time we stopped being jokers on the battlefield and confront the devil head on. Resist the devil and he will flee from your marriage. Cast out and smoke out every agent of the devil from your marriage and they will be sent packing. I see God restoring peace, love, communication, and understanding into your marriage. I see the angel of the Lord persecuting every enemy raised against your marriage. I see God bringing confusion and misunderstanding between your husband and the other woman. You shall have your husband back in Jesus' name. I see that run-away husband coming back to his senses. I see reconciliation and a marriage reunion. I see restoration coming to your marriage. Don't give up, help is on the way.

Bareness

Some bareness can have spiritual root causes. The eggs of a woman, which represents her children, can be sold to witches in the spirit. There was one case where the woman's eggs were stolen from her and sold for nickels when she was only about six years old. Sometimes in intercourse the sperms of her husband would never reach her womb because a Satanic agent had been assigned to collect the sperms in order to prevent pregnancy. Until that spiritual agent is cast out of the relationship no children will ever come from the marriage.

There are some families who have broken their promise to a family god. An ancestor probably went to that god for wealth and promised to sacrifice a goat each year. After that ancestor died the family started to cheat the god instead of goat they took chicken. Overtime that family taught they have become too enlighten by modern knowledge because of education, so they don't even sacrifice the hen or chicken any more to the gods. Well the gods still need the blood sacrifice from the family, so the gods have started running through the family taken what is due them from women in the that family through miscarriage because of the covenant they had established with that great ancestor from the family. Anytime a woman is pregnant in the family and is just near delivery they come for the child and the woman loses the baby through miscarriage. The family gods are both angry and hungry. **Until you discover to recover, the gods will demand their sacrifice from you.** Before the Lord God gave victory to Gideon against the Midianites, God told Gideon to destroy the altar of Baal that was erected by his father. The covenant established by Gideon's father and family god (Baal) had to be broken down first before Gideon could have victory over his enemies. Note here that Gideon had the promise from God to have victory over his enemies but God told him to first destroy the covenant made by his father with Baal. This is a deep spiritual principle and it is important that you understand it. The Bibles says, **"then the LORD turned to him (Gideon), and said, "Go in this might of yours, and you shall save Israel from the hands of the Midianites. Have I not sent you." (Judges 6:14)**

"And the LORD said to him, "Surely I will be with you, and you shall defeat the Midianites as one man." (Judges 6:16)

"Now it came to pass the same night that the LORD said to him, "Take your father's young bull, the second bull of seven years old, and tear down the altar of Baal that your father has, and cut down

the wooden image that is beside it, and build an altar to the LORD your God on top of this rock in the proper arrangement, and take the second bull and offer burnt sacrifice with the wood of image which you shall cut down. So Gideon took ten men from among his servants and did as the LORD had said to him." (Judges 6:25-27)

It is time you used the blood of Jesus in your fasting and prayer to break these curses. I hear the cry of a baby in the house. God is about to intervene and bless you with a child. The curse of bareness is broken in Jesus name. The Bible declares, **"sing, O barren woman, you who never bore a child; burst into songs, shout for joy, you who were never in labor; because more are the children of the desolate woman than of her who has a husband," says the LORD."** (Isaiah 54:1)

Singleness

Some singleness is due to spiritual marriage. When someone often has sex in their dreams it means marriage in the spiritual realms. This can lead to inability to marry, impotence, miscarriages, barrenness, quarrels and hatred between spouses and inability to enjoy sex with ones spouse. Spiritual marriage has to be broken with intensive prayers and the blood of Jesus. When a lady is married spiritually to a family god, any time the lady gets involved in any serious relationship the spirit married to her drives the man away. The woman may do every thing right in the relationship but when she is close to getting married, the man ends up breaking their promise. If, however, the spiritual marriage is not broken by the power of the Holy Spirit and the woman marries, the spirit can influence the marriage to end in divorce in a short time. God said it was not good for Adam to be alone so he brought Eve to Adam. I see God breaking the spiritual marriage and covenant from your life in Jesus' name and bringing the right life partner to you. I see God taking back from the enemy your hidden glory and restoring it into your life. You shall not be disappointed and cheated by men any more in Jesus' name. You shall be happily married and have children in Jesus' name. Get ready O you singles for your hour of divine visitation is here in Jesus' name.

Sickness

Some of the sicknesses we term scientifically as being genetic are actually demonic sicknesses. Some sicknesses are given to people spiritually only to manifest physically. We have what we call **"eaters of flesh and drinkers of blood."**

"When the wicked, even my enemies and my foes came upon me to eat up my flesh, they stumbled and fell." (Psalm 27:2)

Eaters of flesh and drinkers of blood can convert people to all kinds of animals for consumption. They can eat up a person's intestines only for the doctor to diagnose the person and say he/she has stomach ulcer. The Bible declares that the children of darkness are wiser in their ways than the children of light. Satan and his agents are always carrying out researches to find new and clever ways of destroying people. **If you are not born-again believer, filled with the Holy Ghost and fire and you don't know your rights in Christ Jesus, you are an easy prey for eaters of flesh and the drinkers of blood. However, if you are born-again, filled with the Holy Ghost and Fire and you know your rights as a believer you are just untouchable and ' undonatable' for eaters of flesh and drinkers of blood. "And I will feed them that oppress thee with their own flesh. And they shall be drunk with their own blood, as with sweet wine; and all flesh shall know that I the Lord am thy Savior and thy Redeemer, the mighty One of Jacob." (Isaiah 49:26)**

I know of a man who had both liver and kidney problems. When he was spiritually diagnosed by the power of the Holy Spirit, it was discovered that witches in his family had run nails through both organs. He was being killed silently. Many times you see people who are vibrant and very active and then suddenly they are diagnosed with a horrible disease such as cancer and brain tumor. These are all the works of the enemy. I call them **'Silent killers'**. These demons kill people softly spiritually only to manifest in the physical later on. There was this case where a young lady was given HIV/AIDS spiritually by witches in her family. It took the intervention of God to reverse the verdict of the witchcraft plot against her. They had planned to influence her to have sex with a young man carrying the HIV virus. But God intervened and set her free. I see God uprooting every Satanic implantation from your body in Jesus' name. Anything God did not plant in your body but the devil planted in your body dies in Jesus' name. I see your ailing body responding to the word of the Lord. You are healed by the stripes of Jesus. Amen and Amen

Setbacks

Sometimes at the point of a major breakthrough, an individual suddenly loses the chance to be promoted, succeed, and move forward with their lives. We have setback spirits, which fight the destiny of people. Some times you work so hard to save money for a major project only to lose the money to a problem in the family or some tragic incident in the family. It is like any time you gather; the devil comes to scatter your breakthrough. Because of these setbacks some of us have not been able to do anything major in our lives. Houses we planned to build for our families back home are still uncompleted for many years, all due to lack of funds, yet we work so hard. Some of us have been in the US for so long and we have worked so hard but we have nothing to show. Our savings and checking account is empty. We live from paycheck to paycheck. The spirit of retrogression and setbacks can either delay or deny us of our access to our dreams, goals, and breakthroughs. These spirits resolve not to see us prosper, succeed or breakthrough. These spirits can monitor the ways of an individual and whenever that individual is about to breakthrough in life they pull the strings to draw the individual backwards. Setbacks can be in the area of education, finance, business, and marriage. May the Spirit of God break every setback spirit in your life in Jesus' name. May the good Lord favor you and bless you. May the blessing of God cause you to begin to overtake those who have gone ahead of you in Jesus' name.

Short Life

I know of a man who lived his life in fear of dying at the age of forty. He is physically strong, well built, and tall but the fear of untimely death tormented him constantly. The reason being that in his family any time the men got to their late forties they mysteriously died. By the grace of God he was delivered from the spirit of fear and death at the crusade grounds by the power of the Holy Ghost. Some ancestors have exchanged the lives of their people with wealth. People from these families can be very rich but they don't live long to enjoy their wealth. These are all due to the selfish and ignorant actions of some of our ancestors. Some witches and wizards in certain families do not grow old or age because; they donate and replace their bodies and life with other people in the family. **"Since thou was precious in my sight, thou has been honorable, and I have loved thee; therefore, will I give men for thee, and people for thy life."(Isaiah 43:4)**

So, it is very possible to exchange one's life for another. It is important for us to understand that, a spirit of witchcraft can never repent, it can never be pacified. All evil spirits are defying God. They are never going to make peace with God. The Bible says, pray for your enemies, it did not say, pray for demons. Rather we are commanded by our Lord Jesus to cast out demons. Thank God for the blood of Jesus. The blood of Jesus can rectify all these Satanic errors in our families. **You shall not die before your time but rather you shall live and declare the wonderful works of the Lord in your life in Jesus' name. Long life and good health is your portion in Jesus' name.**

Curses

We have four main types of curses that affect people's lives. They are:

1. Self-Imposed Curse
2. Curse of Victimization
3. God's Curse
4. Generational Curse
5. Self-Imposed Curse

Self-imposed curse is when people are cursed by themselves because of their own negative words or confessions. The Bible says that the devil is roaring like a lion seeking for whom he may devour. **"Life and death lies in the power of the tongue and those who love it shall eat the fruit thereof." (Proverb 18:21)**

"For by your words you will be justified, and by your words you will be condemned."(Matthews 12:37) When we use our tongue to say negative words about ourselves, demons pick them up and turn them into curses against us in the future. As Christians, we have to use our tongue to build ourselves and others up and not to curse and pull down people. **We have to be careful what we say, because they will be used against us by the devil and his demons.**

(You have the right to remain silent when under pressure by the devil. Every negative word you say can be used against you by the accuser of the brethren the devil)

Curse of victimization

This type of curse is brought about when people pronounce or speak negative words, pronouncements, and decrees against us. **It can come from parents against their children, wives against their husbands or husbands against their wives, pastors against their members, teachers against their students, etc**. This type of curse usually comes from our enemies who spent their time speaking negative words, pronouncements, and decrees against us to destroy us. An example is when Balak hired the prophet Balaam to curse the children of Israel. **"Then Balak said to him (Balaam), "Please come with me to another place from which you may see them; you shall see only the outer part of them, you shall not see them all; curse them for me from there." (Numbers 23: 13)**

God's Curse

This type of curse is seen in the lives of people who disobey God and continually break God's commandments. These people do not have the fear of God and are bent on doing evil against God and His Children. God's wrath and curse comes upon such people. **"But it shall come to pass, if you do not obey the voice of the LORD your God, to observe carefully all His commandments and His statutes which I command you today that all these curses will come upon you and overtake you." (Deuteronomy 28:15)**

Generational Curse

Generational curses come into our lives by inheritance from our blood line of our parents and ancestors. **The way to discover if you are under any form of a generational curse is when you start experiencing a repeat of the same negative cycles or patterns your family members experienced or is experiencing now. When there is an area in your life which you seem not to be able to overcome because of strange resistance. It is a sign that you are under a curse or that area of your life is cursed. A curse can affect one aspect of your life or affect every aspect of your life.**

Examples of Curses (Not always the case):

1. Poverty: financial insufficiency, lack, debt, always borrowing, bankruptcy, never able to save.

2. Chronic Sickness/Diseases: Hereditary disease, incurable sicknesses, terminal diseases, etc.

3. Repeated failures/Defeat: Always losing to the battles of life, being the tail not the head, being beneath and not above, constant failures and defeat.

4. Marital Spells: Finding it difficult to marry and stay in marriage. Constant conflict and confusion in marriage.

5. Disfavor: People constantly don't take you seriously or respect you. People are suspicious about you without reason; people don't trust you for no reason; people use you and dump you always; people always pay your good with evil; people constantly reject and disappoint you.

6. Limitations: You feel caged, imprisoned, restricted, restrained in life. You feel something is keeping your potentials and destiny down. You have great ideas and dreams but can't express them. You are qualified but always denied. Can't seem to crossover to the next level in your life. You are better than your peers but they are far ahead of you in life.

7. Delay and Lateness: You are late in life. You are behind in many areas of your life. You rise today and fall tomorrow; prolonged breakthrough in every area of your life.

8. Female Problems: Barrenness, miscarriage, menstrual problems, fibroid, impotency, painful menses, painful sexual life.

9. Family Problems: People in the family don't get along, lack of love and trust, child abuse, incest, homosexuality, divorce, separation, alcoholism, poverty, witchcraft, and abuse.

10. Mental/Emotional Breakdown: Nervous breakdown, depression, suicidal thoughts, fear, torment, stress, anxiety, rejection, and self-pity.

11. Accident/Loses: Frequent domestic accidents or injury, work accident, car accident, property damages, loss of job, money, and investments, challenges in school.

Please remember that if you experience any of the mentioned

problems, it doesn't always mean you are under a curse. There is always an exception to the rules. However, if you are constantly experiencing any of these problems, you may want to seek for deliverance from the Lord.

Witchcraft

A lot of people's lives, decision, and choices are controlled, manipulated, influenced, and dominated by witchcraft. Witches work together with demons to destroy the lives of people who are not strong in the Lord. Witches and wizards are flesh eaters and blood drinkers. They are destroyers of lives and destinies. They collaborate with demons to destroy families, churches, marriages, lives, and destinies. A witch or wizard may pretend to be very nice outwardly but in the spirit world, they are very dangerous and destructive. They can come in the form of your best friends, relatives, coworkers and yet possessed by the spirit of witchcraft. **Their job description is to steal, kill, and destroy.** The joy and happiness of witches and wizards is to see lives destroyed, destiny aborted, broken homes, divorces, and wasted lives. It must be noted here that witches and wizards are very committed to their evil works. **If you don't stop them in Jesus' name, they will stop you.**

Spell, Charm and Hexes, Voodoo, Obeah, Sorcery, Divination

Agents in the Satanic kingdom use these weapons to destroy people. **If you are not prayerful and strong in spirit, your enemies can use any of these weapons to destroy your life, marriage, family, dreams, vision, health, career, children, and properties.** What these agents of darkness do is to invoke your spirit into their witchcraft coven and cast a spell or hexes on it and it begin to manifest in your life. Once the spell or charm is cast, your life begins to fall apart. They can also use any thing that belongs to you as a point of contact to cast spell, charm, and hexes against you. Through their spell, voodoo, charm, divination, and obeah, they can affect and afflict every area of your life and finally destroy you. This is why Christians have to constantly soak themselves in the blood of Jesus Christ for divine protection and prayerfully destroy all arsenals against them from the pit of hell.

Satanic Banks and Warehouse

Many individuals' blessings, treasures, fortunes, and prosperities have been stolen by the devil and his cohorts and kept in the demonic banks and warehouse. As a believer, if you don't aggressively pray and command the release of your blessings from the camp of the devil, you will not see the full manifestations of your dreams and visions in life. The Bible talks about binding the strongman and then taking your goods from him.

"In fact, no one can enter a strongman's house and carry off his possession unless he first ties or binds up the strong man then he can rob his house." (Mark 3:27)

Incubus and Succubus (Spiritual Marriage)

This is when an unclean spirits (demonic spirits) from the sea or marine world have sex with people in their dream. These demons rape their victims in their sleep or dreams. They can also entice their victims to have sex with them in their dreams by appearing to be their spouse or boyfriend/girlfriend. **The male demon is called Incubus and the female demon is called Succubus. These demons play a major role in destroying many marriages. They come between husbands and wives. They do this by turning spouses against each other and finally cause separation and divorce. If you do not know how these demons operate, they will cause you to divorce or separate from your God given spouse. They are the mystery behind many broken marriages and relationships. Cast them out in Jesus' name and enjoy your marriage.**

How do people get these demons?

1. Through ancestral covenant with the queen of the coast or marine kingdom.

2. Through your ancestors or parents initiating you to the marine kingdom.

3. Through love spells. People can assign these demons to come into your life.

4. Through sexual transference: fornication, adultery, pornography, lesbianism, clubs, sexual impurity, masturbation, provocative dressing (exposing your body), lust, sexual movies, and sexual songs.

5. Christian couples defiling their marital bed by implementing pornographic worldly ideas into their love life.

Signs and Symptoms of spiritual marriage

- Having sex in your dreams with strangers and animals.
- Seeing yourself under the ocean with strangers.
- Swimming with fish in the sea.
- Getting married in your dreams and also nursing babies in your dreams.

Getting married in your dream

Effect of Spiritual Marriage
Women: (Demon against women Incubus)

- They can block you from getting married.
- They can cause you not to enjoy your marriage.
- They can bring constant confusion and
- misunderstanding between you and your husband.
- They can cause divorce and separation.

- They can hinder you from enjoying sex with your
- spouse due to painful sex with your spouse.
- They can prevent you from getting pregnant.
- They can cause constant miscarriage to your pregnancy.
- They can destroy your finances and career.
- They can cause barrenness.
- They cause stagnation and regression in life
- Hormonal imbalance.
- Growth on sexual organs.
- They can implant fibroid into your womb to block your pregnancy.
- They can cause prolong and painful menstruation.
- They can cause you to hate and disrespect your spouse.
- They can control, manipulate, influence, and dominate your decisions and choices.
- They can give you sickness and diseases

Men: (Demon against men is Succubus)

Men also experience the same problems like the women and these things too.

- Low sperm count.
- Rectal dysfunction (impotence).
- No commitment in relationships or marriage.
- Block men from marrying.
- Prolong marriage.
- Cause men to be very abusive to spouse. Verbal, physical, and emotional abuse from men.
- Hatred, disrespectful, and unforgiving to wives.

- Mental cruelty

- Infidelity

- Uncontrolled anger towards spouse

- Incompatibility with wife.

- Poor communication with wife

- Destroy finances and cause stagnation in life.

- Poor money management.

Foothold and Stronghold

Stronghold can be defined as an area in our lives that is heavily occupied, influenced, and controlled by either God or the devil. There are positive strongholds and negative strongholds.

A positive stronghold is when God becomes your refuge, fortress and strength. When a child of God dwells in His secret place under the shadow of the Almighty God, they dwell in the stronghold of God. The devil cannot touch them nor do them harm. Some Christian responsibilities can become a stronghold in a believer's life. Things such as prayer, reading your Bible, fasting, worship, praise, and holy living can become positive strongholds in a Christian's life. Through these activities they find refuge, protection, provision, sustenance, and confidence in Jesus Christ. Jesus Christ fully becomes their rock, security, and high tower that their enemies cannot overcome them.

"The Lord is my rock, my fortress and my deliverer; my God is my rock, in whom I take refuge. He is my shield and horn of my salvation, my stronghold." (Psalm 18: 2). "The Lord is a refuge for the oppressed, a stronghold in times of trouble." (Psalm 9 vs. 9)

A negative stronghold is when our lives are controlled, manipulated, influenced, and dominated by the flesh, devil and his demons. When a negative stronghold is working in someone's life, the devil puts limitations and restrictions on them. Negative strongholds put an individual in Satan's bondage and oppression. "For though we walk in the flesh, we do not war according to the flesh; for the weapons of our warfare are not carnal but mighty in God for pulling down stronghold." (2 Corinthians 10 vs. 3-4)

"And the king and his men went to Jerusalem against the Jebusites, the inhabitants of the land, who spoke to David, saying, " You shall not come in here; but the blind and the lame will repel you," Nevertheless David took the stronghold of Zion (that is, the city of David)." (2 Samuel 5 vs. 7)

Sin is a major cause of strongholds in many lives. It always starts with a foothold.

A foothold is the first compromise to sin. Once a believer starts compromising with sin, a foothold is established in his/her life. This means that the door is opened for demons to enter into the life of the Christian. It will not be long before demons begin to build their strongholds and establish their throne in a believer's life.

Examples of strongholds:

Destructive addictive behaviors such as alcoholism, drug, addiction, pornography, lust, masturbation, womanizing, gossip, lying, stealing, fear, depression, worry, anxiety, insomnia, post-traumatic stress disorder, etc.

Other ways strongholds can be established in our lives are by generational curses and occultic involvements.

Jesus Christ has come to deliver you and me from every form of Satanic stronghold. You can deliver yourself from the stronghold of the devil by repenting from your sins and binding every strongman holding you in captivity by the power of the Holy Spirit in Jesus name. "In fact, no one can enter a strongman's house and carry off his possession unless he first ties or binds up the strong man then he can rob his house." (Mark 3 vs. 27)

Evil Foundation

An evil foundation is when your bloodline or family tree is cursed and therefore, the curse has the ability to affect members of that family if not broken in Jesus' name. The word of the Lord says, **"If the foundation is destroyed, what can the righteous do." (Psalm 11 vs. 3)** The practice of false religion, idolatry, and occultic activities establishes evil foundations in people's lives and family. **The good news is that when you become a born-again Christian, the precious blood of Jesus Christ redeems you from generational curses. The precious blood of Jesus Christ is our ransom, the price that was paid for our liberty and freedom from the bondage of the devil.**

These scriptures found below, prove that under the new covenant with the precious blood of Jesus Christ, family tree, or generational curses do not have power over your life. You just have to know the truth which will set you free. The word of the Lord declares,

"Fathers shall not be put to death for their children. Nor children be put to death for their fathers. Each is to die for his own sin." (Deuteronomy 24 vs. 16)

"What do you people mean by quoting this proverb about the Land of Israel. "The fathers eat sour grapes, and the children's teeth are set on edge." (Ezekiel 18: 2)

"In those days they shall no longer say, "The fathers have eaten sour grapes, and the children's teeth are set on edge." (Jeremiah 31: 29)

The above scriptures prove that under the new covenant, the born-again believer shouldn't be under generational or inherited curses of their ancestors and parents.

Python Spirit and Leviathan Demon

The python spirit is a serpentine demon that swallows destinies and squeezes life out of people. This demon is responsible for causing unfulfilled dreams and visions. **Leviathan** is a giant serpentine sea creature. They cause delay, stagnation, and retrogression in life. They limit, constrain, and restrict people's potentials. They cause fatigue and weakness to their victims. They systematically drain life and hope from people. They destroy people emotionally with fear, depression, anxiety, stress, panic, and sleeplessness. They render their victims hopeless and helpless.

They swallow up people's breakthrough, fortunes, riches, prosperity and health. They block people from growing spiritually by hindering their prayer life, Bible studies, faith, and fasting life. Their victims begin to find it very difficult to obey God. They try to disconnect their victims from the Holy Spirit.

Asmodeus and Osmodeus

These are marriage-breaking principalities and demons that cause singleness and divorce. They war against marriages to destroy it by causing divorce and separation. They prevent singles from getting married. They take marriage couples captives and turn couples against each other. They convince singles that they don't need a soul mate, yet cause them lust after the opposite sex behind the scenes or burn in passion. They put obstacles before singles who attempt to marry by breaking every healthy relationship leading to marriage. They break existing, and longstanding relationships.

Satanic Spider Web and Net

Satanic webs and nets are weapons used by witchcraft and demons to entrap people to destroy them. Once the net or web is cast on you, you begin to sense the spirit of heaviness and you become entangled. Things begin to go bad in your life once the witchcraft web or net is in operation. Your enemies can begin to attack you in every area of your life once you have been trapped by the web or net in the spirit world. You become vulnerable in the hands of your enemies when the net or web is released against you. All good things are blocked from coming into your life. You will begin to experience frustration and limitation in your life. They render you hopeless and helpless. You become stranded in life with no progress and success coming your way.

Satanic Monitors

A lot of people are being closely monitored by their enemies. Their enemies use psychic computers, magical mirrors, demonic antennas, and witchcraft searchlight discs to monitor their movement. Once your enemies are able to monitor your life through these mediums, they can easily destroy every good thing that comes your way. They can block you from receiving or coming into contact with your breakthroughs.

Satanic monitors can also come in the form of animals, artifacts in our homes, and even people around us. These are called secret agent with secret mission to collect information from you for your destruction. The work of the Satanic monitors or secret agents is to gather relevant information about you so that your enemies can use it against your progress and success in life. This is why you have to be very careful who you share your secret or vital information with. The devil can even use close friends, and relatives to get information from you and then use it to block your breakthrough and progress in life. **Watch and pray so that the Holy Spirit will deliver you from Satanic monitors**.

Evil Altars and Covenants

We have people who are presently facing spiritual problems because of a covenant they established with the devil directly or indirectly by getting themselves involved in Satanic activities, occultic rituals and secret societies. When people dabble with psychic, mediums, sorority, fraternity, palm reading, witchcraft, voodoo, obeah and sorcery, they have made a covenant with the devil. The devil can use their visit or practice of these things as a point of contact to afflict and destroy them. An altar is a place where Satanic agents make their sacrifices to demons or idols. It is the meeting place between the humans and the demons. When you or your ancestors sacrifice anything to demons or idols, an evil covenant is established and it gives access to the demons to come into the family to afflict and destroy the destinies of the people in that family.

Evil Soul Ties

Some married couples are having problems in their marriage because of soul-tie. When you become very intimate with someone and later break the relationship, there can be a soul tie bond which can leave your soul fragmented. You will find it difficult to move on into another healthy relationship because part of your ex-boyfriend/ex-girlfriend soul is still lingering in your soul. You can move on to marry but you will find yourself still desiring your former ex- boyfriend/ex-girlfriend. This is the reason why God warns us not to have sex before marriage and sex outside of marriage. When we have sex before or outside of marriage, we sin against our own soul. You need to break every soul tie with all the people you had sex with before or after marriage for your total deliverance. You do this by repenting and renouncing your relationship with them.

Familiar and Ancestral Spirits

These demons are from our blood line and they keep records of all covenants established by our ancestors with the devil. They go through the family tree and make sure that people inherit blood transferred generational curses. These demons enforce generational curses and stronghold on members of the family carrying the ancestry genes or blood.

Body Affliction

These demons are released by witches or Satanic agent to afflict people in their body. They can come in the form of heat sensation in your body, animals crawling on your body, movement inside of your body, hearing voices, seeing things that others cannot see, and forgetting things. These things can begin to happen to a person under a curse, spell, and a hex.

Demonic Visitations

This is when demons are released to haunt a person's house or life. You see or feel demonic presence in your house like shadows, animals, scent, voices, and writings. People sometime hear the audible voices of these demons but others cannot hear the voice. You see them but other cannot see them. You see them following you everywhere you go and also in your dreams. This is called demonic visitation.

Witchcraft Scapegoat

This comes to play when a member of a particular family is donated to demons or household witchcraft for destruction after a member of the family makes a covenant with demons or idols. Usually the first born of the family is donated. When this happens, all the other children succeed in life except the first born donated. Any member of the family can be donated for destruction. Just make sure you are not a scapegoat for any household wickedness.

Star Hunters

In the secular world, we have people who we refer to as stars. These stars are admired, adored and even worshiped by their fans. They are called stars because of their success and achievement in a particular field. Stars manage to express or manifest their God given talents, skills and potential to the fullness. Their stars shine so bright that people come and bask in their glory. In the world of music, Michael Jackson is the king of Pop music. Michael Jordan, Tiger woods, Mohammed Ali are all stars in the world of sports. In the world of politics we have names such as George Washington, Abraham Lincoln, Nelson Mandela, Kwame Nkrumah and Gandhi who are all stars because of what they did for their countries.

It is very important for us to understand that God has created all of us to be stars to glorify Him. As children of God, God expect us to glorify Him with our stars. **The question here is who do men use their stardom to glorify?** Is it themselves, God or Satan. It is equally important for us to understand that God has given each of us gifts, talent, skill, knowledge, and wisdom in a measure to glorify Him. When we invest our talents, skills, gifts, knowledge, and wisdom into His kingdom, God doubles His anointing and blessing on us to do much more.

"A certain nobleman went into a far country to receive for himself a kingdom and to return. So he called ten of his servants, delivered to them ten minas, and said to them, **'Do business till I come.'** But his citizens hated him, and sent a delegation after him, saying, 'We will not have this man to reign over us.' And so it was that when he returned, having received the kingdom, he then commanded these servants, to whom he had given the money, to be called to him, **that he might know how much every man had gained by trading.** Then came the first, saying, 'Master, your minas has **earned ten minas.'** And he said to him, well done, good servant; because you were faithful in a very little, have authority over ten cities. And the second came, saying, 'Master, your minas **has earned five minas.'** Likewise he said to him, 'You also be over five cities.' **Then another came, saying, 'Master, here is your minas, which I have kept put away in a handkerchief. For I feared you, because you are an austere man. You collect what you did not sow. 'And he said to him, Out of your own mouth I will judge you, you wicked servant. You knew that I was an austere man, collecting what I did not deposit and reaping what I did not sow. Why then did you not put my money in the bank, that at my coming I might have collected it with interest?' And he said to those who stood by, 'Take the minas from him, and give it to him who has ten minas.' (But they said to him, 'Master, he has ten minas.) For I say to you, that to everyone who has will be given; and** from him who does not have, even what he has will be taken away from him." (Luke 19:12-26)

Sometimes when people get to the top and their stars are shining so bright, they begin to think that it is by their own wisdom, hard work, and principles that they have attained their success and glory. They begin to make themselves gods and do not give the glory to the Almighty God. What we have to remember is that if God does not give us breath to live how can we ever become anything or achieve anything. God knows just what to do to humble the proud. The Bible declares,

"The ground of a certain rich man yielded plentifully. And he thought within himself, saying, 'What shall I do, since I have no room to store my crops?' So he said, 'I will do this: I will pull down my barns and build greater, and there I will store all my crops and my goods. And I will say to my soul, "Soul, you have many good laid up for many years; take your ease, eat, drink, and be merry." But God said to him, 'Fool! This night your soul will be required of you; then whose will those things be which you have provided?' "So is he who lays up treasures for himself, and is not rich toward God." (Luke 12:16- 21)

"Now King Herod had been very angry with the people of Tyre and Sidon; but they came to him with one accord, and having made Blastus the king's personal aide their friends, they asked for peace, because their country was supplied with food by the king's country. So on a set day Herod, arrayed in royal apparel, sat on his throne and gave an oration to them, And the people kept shouting, "The voice of a god and not a man!" Then immediately an angel of the Lord struck him (Herod), because he did not give glory to God. And he was eaten by worms and died." (Act 12:20-23)

"All this came upon King Nebuchadnezzar. At the end of the twelve months he was walking about the royal palace of Babylon. The king spoke, saying, "Is not this great Babylon, that I have built for a royal dwelling by my mighty power and for the honor of my majesty?" (Daniel 4:28) While the word was still in the king's mouth, a voice fell from heaven:

"King Nebuchadnezzar, to you it is spoken: the kingdom has departed from you! And they shall drive you from men, and your dwelling shall be with the beasts of the field. They shall make you eat grass like oxen; and seven times shall pass over you, until you know that the Most High rules in the kingdom of men, and gives it to whomever He chooses." "That very hour the word was fulfilled concerning Nebuchadnezzar; he was driven from men and ate grass like oxen; his body was wet with the dew of heaven till his hair had grown like eagles' feathers and his nails like birds claws." (Daniel 4:28-33)

Nebuchadnezzar was the greatest King in his generation but because of his pride God demoted him and turned him into a beast for seven years. However, when he repented and recognized that God was to be given all the glory and honor, his kingdom was restored unto him. The Bible declares, "and at the end of the time I, Nebuchadnezzar, lifted my eyes to heaven, and my understanding returned to me; and I blessed the Most High and praised and honored Him who lives forever: For His dominion is an everlasting dominion, And His kingdom is from generation to generation. All the inhabitants of the earth are reputed as nothing; He does according to His will in the army of heaven and among the inhabitants of the earth. No one can restrain His hand or say to Him," what have you done?" At the same time my reason returned to me, and for the glory of my kingdom, my honor and splendor returned to me. My counselors and nobles resorted to me, I was restored to my kingdom, and excellent majesty was added to me. Now I, Nebuchadnezzar, praised and extol and honor the King of heaven, all of whose works are truth, and His ways justice. And those who walk in pride He is able to put down." (Daniel 4:36 - 37)

Jacob understood the mystery of stars in the Old Testament. He knew that his twelve sons were all stars. However, Josephs star was brighter than his other eleven brothers. The Bible declares:

"Then he (Joseph) dreamed still another dream and told it to his brothers, and said, **"Look, I have dreamed another dream. And this time, the sun, the moon, and the eleven stars bowed down to me."** So he told it to his father and his brothers; and his father rebuked him and said to him, "What is this dream that you have dreamed? Shall your **mother** (moon) and **I (Sun)**, and your **brothers (Stars)** indeed come to bow down to the earth before you?" And his brothers envied him, but his father kept the matter in mind." (Genesis 37: 9-11)

Jesus Christ is the greatest star of all stars. His star is bigger and brighter than any star. It is written, "Now after Jesus was born in Bethlehem of Judea in the days of Herod the king, behold, wise men from the East came to Jerusalem, saying, "Where is He who has been born King of the Jews? For we have seen **His star in the East and have come to worship Him."** (Matthew 2:1-2)

We have what is called **Star Hunters**. The greatest star hunter is Satan and his mission is to kill, steal, and destroy. Satan has also employed his cohorts and human agent to hunt down people's stars and stop their stars from shinning to magnify God. Star hunters will do their best to prevent you from achieving your goals and purpose in life. Star hunters pursue people's destiny. Their chief agenda is to kill, steal and destroy your dreams and vision in life. Star hunters will try to kill you before you manifest your God given purpose in life. Such was the case of **Jesus** and **Moses.** Satan worked through **Herod** and **Pharaoh** to kill Jesus and Moses respectively when they were only babies. But thank God for divine intervention. God always reveals to redeem his children whose ears are attentive to his still small voice. God revealed to Joseph and the wise men the evil intentions of Herod and instructed them as to how to escape the evil traps of Herod.

It is very important for us to understand that the wise men with all their human wisdom and intelligence could not discern or know the wicked plans of Herod. It took God to reveal to the wise men in a dream the evil plan of Herod against the Baby Jesus. We have to note here that it takes the Holy Ghost to know the evil plans of the devil against us. Without the Holy Spirit we will became victims to the traps of the enemy.

When star hunters do not succeed in killing you, they will resolve to destroy you by putting obstacles in your way so that you don't fulfill your dreams and visions in life. **Star hunter will use Satanic problems to distract you from pursuing your purpose in life.** A typical example is the woman with issue of blood in the Bible. She spent all her life and wealth battling her sickness and did not have time to discover and pursue her dreams in life. Star hunters will try to delay and deny you your purpose in life.

Even when you overcome all the barriers and make it to the top, star hunters will always be around to pull you down and cause you to fail. Jesus was always surrounded by star hunters. Jesus' star hunters were the Pharisees, Sadducees, and the Teachers of the law. They were always looking for a way to destroy Jesus. The star hunter for David is King Saul. King Saul wanted to kill David at all cost and stop David's star from ever shinning. With Joseph, his own eleven brothers were his star hunter. The devil will use any thing and every thing he has to try and stop ones star from shinning. Apostle Paul was a star of the gospel of our Lord Jesus Christ. He also had star hunters who wanted to stop him at all cost. The Bible declares:

"And when it was day, some of the Jew banded together and bound themselves under an oath, saying that they would neither eat nor drink till they had killed Paul. Now there were more than forty who had formed this conspiracy. They came to the chief priests and elders, and said, "We have bound ourselves under a great oath that we will eat nothing until we have killed Paul." (Acts 23:12-14)

Star Hunters don't play they are serious with their mission to destroy our stars. Satan can use women, men, money, pride, and drugs to cause one to fall from glory. Today it is not surprising that a lot of stars are being destroyed by drugs, sexual scandals, character assassination, and money problems. As you can see, star hunters can be employed by Satan from any area of your life to destroy your star from shinning. He can use your own moral weakness, friends, family relations, business partners, and unseen agents to destroy you. **Our only hope of escaping the snares of star hunters is a close relationship with Jesus. He is the only one who can protect us from the traps of the enemy.** Jesus Christ said, **"no one can enter a strong man's house and plunder his goods, unless he first binds the strong man. And then he will plunder his house."(Mark 3: 27)**

The truth of the matter is that most of the problems listed above are brought about by wicked spiritual strong men. These wicked strong men are rulers who do not want to lose their control over their clients. They do not easily free their captives. The only way we can break ourselves from their oppression is by being violent in the spirit. **You have to receive anointing from God through the power of the Holy Ghost in Jesus' name to become stronger than them before you can break away from their evil influence on your life.** The Bible declares, **"it shall come to pass in that day. That his burden will be taken away from your shoulder, and his yoke from your neck and the yoke will be destroyed because of the anointing oil." (Isaiah 10:27)**

Without the power of the Holy Ghost we don't stand the chance of defeating the strongman in our lives. Jesus said, **"This kind can come out by nothing but prayer and fasting." (Mark 9:29)**

The strongman behind some of our problems can only be bound and plundered **only through fasting and praying.** Some times prayer alone is not enough to bind and plunder the strongman. We have to have a combination of fasting and aggressive prayers to be able to bind and cast the strongman out of our lives. A typical example of a strong man who oppressed God's children is Pharaoh. The Bible declares, **"afterward Moses and Aaron went in and told Pharaoh, "Thus says the LORD God of Israel: 'Let My people go, that they may hold a feast to Me in the wilderness." And Pharaoh said, "Who is the LORD that I should obey His voice to let Israel go? I do not know the LORD, nor will let Israel go." (Exodus 5:1-2)**

The strongman, Pharaoh who is the wicked force behind your

problem is saying that he doesn't know why he should let you become pregnant, married, rich, healthy, and shine in life. Until you continue to mount the pressure through fasting and prayer, he will not let you go. Some Christians are too nice, courteous, kind, gentle, professional and diplomatic when they are dealing with the devil. They have no idea the stubborn enemy they are up against. They don't know that the **devil is wickedly wicked and badly bad**. The only language he understands is **force, aggression, and resistance**. That is why the Bible says that **resist the devil and he will flee from you**.

When the man of God, Smith Wigglesworth was asked why he dealt with the devil forcefully when doing ministrations, he said he believed that Satan should never be treated gently or allowed to get away with anything. Until you show Pharaoh the raw power of God he will keep you in bondage. **Don't you ever compromise with Pharaoh just disconnect yourself from him by being holy and then bombard him with the lethal weapons of warfare in aggressive prayers fueled with fasting and you will be free to inherit your promise land in Jesus' name.** I see you coming out of every Satanic cage in Jesus' name. I see you breaking free from every spiritual slavery and bondage in Jesus' name. I see you coming out of your Egypt by the power of the Holy Ghost in Jesus' name.

Please stop here and make these declarations by faith in Jesus' name. What you bind on earth will be bound in heaven and what you release on earth will be released in heaven. The choice is in your hands. (Life and Death rest in the power of the tongue)

Breakthrough Prayers

I receive a new anointing from God to destroy the works of the enemy in Jesus' name.

I take authority in the name of Jesus and bind principalities, powers, rulers of darkness, spiritual wickedness in high places, and demonic influence in Jesus' name.

I bind every spirit of disobedience and rebellion controlling my children and I command the release of the spirit of love, obedience, and submission in Jesus' name.

I bind every spirit of misunderstanding, contention, fighting, unforgiveness in my marriage and I command the release of love, unity, understanding, forgiveness and peace in my marriage in Jesus' name.

I command the spirit of healing, health, and deliverance from the powers of darkness in Jesus' name.

I redeem back those blessings that the devil has stolen from me in Jesus' name.

I command the restoration of my marriage and family in Jesus' name.

I command every curse that has been in operation over my life to be reversed in Jesus' name.

I break the power and influence of every curse over my life and my family in Jesus' name.

I turn every curse into blessing in my life in Jesus' name.

I release my body, soul and spirit from every python spirit squeezing life and strength out of me in Jesus' name.

I release the fire of God to consume every Satanic gathering being held for my downfall.

I break every Satanic altars erected for my destruction in Jesus' name.

I break every spirit of separation and divorce in my marriage in Jesus' name.

I pray for the salvation of my spouse and family members in Jesus' name.

I cast out every sickness from my body in Jesus' name.

I command my healing and deliverance in Jesus' name.

I take authority in Jesus' name and cut off the head of the python spirit by the sword of the spirit in Jesus' name.

I command the release of my children from the influence of peer pressure in Jesus' name.

I take authority in the name of Jesus and bind every disobedient spirit in my children.

I take authority in Jesus' name and release my sons and daughters from every bad behavior.

I break the influence of the enemy over my children and my spouse in Jesus' name.

I command the release of love, peace, understanding, and communication between me and my spouse in Jesus' name.

I command the deliverance of my spouse from every pornographic spirit, womanizing spirit, alcoholic, and cigarette habits in Jesus' name.

I break the influence and the operations of any demon causing my spouse to mistreat me in Jesus' name.

I cut off any human agent giving my spouse bad advice in Jesus' name.

I command my spouse and my children to come back to their senses in Jesus' name.

I command the release of a good job to me in Jesus' name.

I bind any strong man preventing me from getting a good job in Jesus' name.

I arrest any demon spirit causing me to waste my money in Jesus' name.

I command the release of financial breakthrough in Jesus' name.

I command the release of marital breakthrough in Jesus' name.

I command the release of fruitfulness in my life in Jesus' name.

I am blessed of God because of Jesus and I cannot be under any Satanic curse.

I command every power of the enemy over my life and my family to be broken in Jesus' name.

I take authority in Jesus' name over every Satanic domination and influence over my life.

I release myself from the stronghold of demons and Satanic influence in Jesus' name.

I am breaking through in Jesus' name into the dimension of the miraculous.

I refuse to be stopped by Satanic limitation and confinements.

I command every limitation and demonic imprisonment to be broken in Jesus' name.

I breakout from every limitation and confinement in Jesus' name.

I arrest and bind every evil spirit and demon that is operating a curse against me in Jesus' name.

My soul has escape from the snare of the enemy. The snare is broken and I have escaped in Jesus' name.

My soul has escaped from the spirit of untimely death in Jesus' name.

My soul has escaped from every form of accident in Jesus' name.

I am kept by the Power of God in Jesus' name.

How to Use the Anointing Oil

The olive or anointing oil in itself is just ordinary oil. What makes it different is the prayers that is prayed on it as a point of contact. So don't put your faith in the oil but in our Lord Jesus Christ who is the anointed one.

Once the oil is prayed on, it is consecrated or set apart to do extraordinary things in the name of our Lord Jesus Christ. The power of the Holy Spirit is spoken into it to do signs and wonders in Jesus' name.

Isaiah 10 vs. 27 says, by the anointing oil the yoke shall be broken.

Mark 6:13 says the disciples of Jesus Christ anointed the sick people and healed them

James 5:14 says, if anyone is sick let him call the elders they will anoint him and the prayer of faith will heal him.

In the Old Testament the anointing oil was used to consecrate or set apart things for God.

You are going to use the anointing oil for blessing, favor, and also to destroy the plans of the enemy against you and your family.

1. When you need favor, after you have prayed to God for favor anoint yourself before an interview. (Psalms 5:12)

2. Periodically anoint your house, car and yourself and cover yourself under the blood of Jesus Christ. Cover yourself with the blood of Jesus every day before stepping out. You don't need the oil to do that.

3. Anoint the place of work against enemies who will try to get you out. Be professional in doing this lest someone think you are doing voodoo at the work place. Use wisdom

4. Anoint your car and yourself when traveling to prevent accident. When people bring you gift anoint it to be a blessing and to destroy every witchcraft activities.

5. When sick, anoint yourself and pray in Jesus name rebuke the sickness.

You say something like this: In the name of Jesus Christ, I anoint myself for divine favor as I go for this interview I claim victory and success by the reason of this anointing in Jesus' name.

In the name of Jesus Christ, I anoint myself, house, children, possession, work place, and cover them under the blood of Jesus Christ. No weapon formed against me and my family shall prosper and every lips, curse, spells, sorcery, and divination against me I destroy them in Jesus name.

Anointing Oil Prayers

Anoint your forehead or face, neck and shoulder and declare these things with authority and faith in Jesus' name. (Isaiah 10: 27)

I am redeemed from the curse of the Law

(Galatians 3: 13) In Jesus name and by the power of the Holy Spirit, I break all generational spirits, curse, spell, sorcery, strongman that came into my life during conception, in the womb in the birth canal, and through the umbilical cord to come out in Jesus' name.

In Jesus' name and by the power of the Holy Spirit, I break all spoken curses and negative words that have been spoken against my life in Jesus' name.

I break all marital spell against my life in Jesus' name.

I take back my glory from the witches in Jesus' name

I destroy the demonic influence over my marital life in Jesus' name.

I break myself loose from demonic yoke in Jesus' name.

By the anointing of the Holy Spirit, I destroy every marine witchcraft burden place in my life in the name of Jesus because I have been redeemed by the blood of Jesus.

By the anointing of the Holy Spirit, I break myself free from every marine witchcraft yoke placed upon my life.

By the reason of the anointing, I command every demonic and witchcraft yoke to be broken over my life in Jesus' name.

By the anointing of the Holy Spirit, I repel every evil spirit away from my life and house in Jesus' name.

I soak my body, soul and spirit under the covering of the protection of the blood of Jesus Christ.

I break every spell, curse, and divination against my life in Jesus' name by the anointing of the Holy Ghost.

Deliverance: Need to Know

Demons

Demons are spiritual persons without bodies. The ratio of humans and demons is about 1 to 1000. For every one human, we have about thousand demons. Demons have different function or responsibilities.

The two main functions of demons

To prevent people from receiving Jesus Christ into their lives as their Lord and personal savior.

To prevent people from serving the Lord and worship Him in truth and in spirit.

Some activities of demons:

Enslave	- harass	- deceive
Defile	- entice	- suppress

Other functions of Demons:

Fornication, adultery, lust, pride, disobedient, suicide, depression, fear, oppression, rejection, depression, infirmities, death, lying, torment, sickness/diseases, unforgiveness, pornography, masturbation, unbelief, confusion, doubt, alcoholism, addictions, violence, evil thought, gossip etc.

Some demons are more powerful than others. Demons love to live in human's body and soul so as to afflict them with their characteristics. Demons can also live in animals and objects when they don't find human residence. **"When an unclean spirit (demon) goes out of a man, he goes through dry places, seeking rest, and finds none. Then he says,' I will return to my house from which I came.' And when he comes, he finds it empty, swept, and put in order. Then he goes and takes with him seven other spirits more wicked than himself, and they enter and dwell there; and the last state of that man is worse than the first." (Matthew 12:43-45)**

This scripture reveals a lot about the nature of demons. This is a breakdown of what this scripture means.

1. **When an unclean spirit (demon) goes out of a man:** This proves that demons love to live in human body. Demons are always looking for an opportunity or an opening to enter into the human body, soul and spirit. Demons will only go out of their victims through **aggression and pressure of the Holy Ghost in Jesus' name.** When you submit to God by obeying Him and you resist the demons, then they will flee from you. Demons are very stubborn tenants and will only succumb to serious aggressive prayer in Jesus' name. They bow to the name of Jesus Christ and are afraid of the blood of Jesus Christ. Once you exercise your authority in Jesus name, they will obey. Before demons obey you, you have to live a holy and righteous life. You have to be full of the Holy Spirit and the word of God.

2. **He goes:** This proves that demons are persons without bodies. They move around.

3. **Goes through dry places:** Dry places represent people who are not filled with the word of God and the Holy Spirit. When Jesus Christ is not Lord and savior over your life, you become an easy prey for demons to enter.

4. **Then he says:** This shows us that demons have mouth and can speak. Demons are the ones who have been whispering evil thoughts or thoughts of evil into our minds. They are the unseen force that tells or suggest to people to commit suicide,

fornicate, murder, hate, lie, and do all manner of evil things.

5. **I will return to my house from which I came:** Demons have memory and they recollect their human residence. They see the human body, soul and spirit as their house. This is the reason why it is sometime difficult to cast out demons from people. When you open the door of sin for them to come in, it becomes difficult to cast them out. This is because they claim ownership to your body.

6. **He finds it empty, swept and put in order:** This happens when a person receives deliverance and demons are cast out of them. They become empty of demons and their body is swept clean and put in order. However, casting out a demon out of a person is not enough. The person who receives the deliverance must make Jesus Christ their Lord and Savior. They have to fill their empty body with the word of God and Holy Spirit. **I advise anyone who is seeking deliverance to spend quality time reading, memorizing, meditating, and obeying the word of God. Failure to do these things is setting yourself up for serious spiritual attacks by stronger and wicked demons.**

7. **Then he goes and takes with him seven other spirits more wicked than himself, and they enter and dwell there:** This is the reason why it is very dangerous to seek for deliverance if you are not a Christian or you are a Christian who hasn't made Jesus Christ your Lord in every area of your life. If you are not fully committed to Jesus Christ and you seek for deliverance, you will leave your body empty of the word of God and the Holy Spirit and it will give way to seven more wicked demons in addition with the first one which was cast out of you to come back to torment and afflict you. **If you are not ready to serve Jesus Christ, then don't seek for deliverance because you will only make your situation worse.** Demons network with each other and they are able to invite stronger demons to come in to help them stay in their human body.

7 Portals of Demonic Entry

There are seven major ways demons get access into people's body. Portal means doorway, entrance, or gateway. The seven portals are:

Eyes   - Mouth   - Nose

Ears   - Skin pores   - Genital

Anal

Eyes: Demons can get into your body by the filthy things you watch or see. Remember demons are spirit without bodies. They are like the smoke, vapor or air and can easily penetrate into the body.

Examples: Horror movies (Harry potter), violent movies, pornographic movies and books, lustful looking at the opposite sex, reading demonic literatures or books

Mouth: Demons can enter into people through their mouths. When we eat things sacrificed to idols or demons. Drinking alcoholic beverages and also smoking allows demons to enter through the mouth.

Nose: Demons are able to enter into our body through our nostrils. When people breathe in air from demonic charged environments such as Satanic temples and shrines. There are some places where the atmosphere is charged with demons. Example is the club, casinos, nude place, visiting the psychic, and shrines. Some people also pick up these demons by breathing in special demonic candles, incense, and perfumes etc.

Ears: Demons can penetrate through our ears into our body by the demonic songs or worldly song we listen to. These music or Satanic messages carry demons with them into our body, soul, and spirit.

Skin Pores: Demons are able to enter through our skin pores through evil incisions on our body, tattoos, body piercing, and drug injections.

Genitals: This is a major entry point for demons. Demons love things relating to sex. They can enter through ungodly sexual intercourse such as fornication, adultery, masturbation, homosexuality, lesbianism, sexual perversion, and impurities.

Anal: Goes for people who practice sexual perversion like homosexuality and lesbianism.

As Christians, we have to protect these seven entry point by staying away from worldly and Satanic materials that contaminate, pollute, defile and make us filth before God.

"Do not be unequally yoked together with unbelievers. For what fellowship has righteousness with lawlessness? And what communion has light with darkness? And what accord has Christ with Belial? Or what part has a believer with an unbeliever? And what agreement has the temple of God with idols? For you are the temple of the living God. As God has said: I will dwell in them and walk amongst them. I will be their God, and they shall be My people. Therefore come out from among them and be separate, says the Lord. Do not touch what is unclean, and I will receive you. I will be a Father to you and you shall be My sons and daughters, says the LORD Almighty." (2 Corinthians 6 vs.14-18)

Other ways demons come into people's lives:

By inheritance: When children inherit demon through mother's placenta or umbilical tube. This is called blood-transferred demons. Example is the spirit of rejection and generational curses transferred from parents to children.

"The LORD is longsuffering and abundant in mercy, forgiving iniquity and transgression; but He by no means clears the guilty, visiting the iniquity of the fathers on the children to the third and fourth generation." (Numbers 14 vs. 18)

Occultic Background: When a person inherit demons from a family where ancestors and parents worshiped Satan and demons. The Bible says, **"When you come into the land which the LORD your God is giving you, you shall not learn to follow the abominations**

of those nations. There shall not be found among you anyone who makes his son or his daughter pass through the fire, or one who practices witchcrafts, or a soothsayer, or who interprets omens, or a sorcerer, or one who conjures spells, or a medium, or a spiritist, or one who calls upon the dead. For all who do these things are an abomination to the LORD, and because of these abominations the LORD your God drives them out from before you." (Deuteronomy 18 vs. 9 to 12)

Personal involvement with occult: When people get demons from dabbling into occultic activities. Examples are psychic, palm reading, witchcraft etc.

Traumatic event: People can get demons through traumatic situations like rape and abuse. Demons take advantage of the traumatic event and enter into the victim's body when they become vulnerable after the abuse or rape.

Areas Controlled by Demons

Emotions: Fear, worry, anxiety, depression, rejection, despair, self-pity, misery, pride, jealousy, loneliness, rebellion, resentment, bitterness, hatred, violence, unforgiveness, and selfishness.

Mind: doubt, unbelief, confusion, indecision, insanity, and evil thought.

Tongue: lying, gossip, criticism, slandering, blasphemy, exaggeration, and cursing.

Sex: sexual perversion, homosexuality, uncleanness, masturbation, pornography, abortion, adultery, and immorality.

Religion and occult: Any religion outside of true Christianity (false religions).

Can a Christian be possessed by Demons?

A true born-again Christian who is filled with the Holy Spirit and the word of God cannot be possessed by demons. Possession means to be completely taken over and controlled by demons. This cannot happen to a true born-again Christian. This is because the born-again Christian is supposed to be possessed by the Holy Spirit.

However, a backsliding Christian who has fallen from the grace and is living in sin can be possessed by demons. At that point they are really not Christians but ex-Christians. Until they repent and turn back to God their going to heaven is even questionable. Many true Christians are demonized. **Demonized means an area of your life is controlled by a demon and you don't have total control over that area of your own life. Examples are unforgiveness, addiction to drugs, lust, anger, gluttony, compulsive behaviors, and alcoholism etc.**

Demonized Christians find it very difficult to mature in the faith and enjoy the peace of God. They have to get the demons out of that area of their life being occupied by the demon. Most true Christians need deliverance from the spirit of unforgiveness, anger, lying, gossip, rejection, self-pity, fear, hate, lust, depression, addiction etc.

How to be delivered

If you need deliverance in any area of your life, be humble and seek for help. Remember pride goes before fall. You have to get rid of your pride and dignity if you need deliverance.

- Be honest about your past life and seek for deliverance.
- Confess all your sins to God. (Proverb 28 vs. 13)
- Repent from all your sins.
- Break away from occultic or secret societies and evil relationship.
- Forgive all persons who have offended you.
- Submit to God and resist the demons and they will flee from you in the mighty name of Jesus Christ. Seek for help if need

be. **(look for a deliverance minister or ministry for help)**

"Therefore submit to God. Resist the devil and he will flee from you." (James 4 vs.7)

"Behold, I give you the authority to trample on serpents and scorpions, and over all the power of the enemy, and nothing shall by any means hurt you." (Luke 10 vs. 19)

"And these signs will follow those who believe: In My name they will cast out demon, they will speak with new tongues; they will take up serpents; and if they drink anything deadly, it will by no means hurt them; they will lay hands on the sick, and they will recover."

Reason Why Some People are Not Delivered

- Lack of repentance
- Lack of desperation (passivity)
- Holding on to wrong relationships
- Wrong motives (getting deliverance without making Jesus Christ their Lord and personal savior)
- Failure to confess a specific sin
- Failure to disconnect yourself from occultic groups or wrong relationships
- When a person is under a curse
- Not making Jesus Lord
- Pride and holding on to their dignity
- Lack of total transparency (Not being honest about your past life and wrong doings)
- Lack of faith in Jesus Christ as your deliverer
- Taking your eyes of Jesus Christ during deliverance. (Look unto Jesus Christ as your sole deliverer)
- Maintaining occultic or demonic object or items in your

possession or home (e.g. rings, amulet, talisman, candles, incense, pictures, music cd, artifact, etc.)

How to Maintain your Deliverance

- Making Jesus Christ your Lord and personal Savior

- Be holy and righteous

- Avoid wrong association

- Consecrate yourself to God

- Read, meditate and obey the Bible

- Be filled with the Holy Spirit

- Submit to God and resist the devil

- Put on the full armor of God.

- Be in fellowship with other believers.

- Fasting and prayers

- Connecting to a deliverance ministry

- Engaging in warfare prayers.

Special note: Deliverance is a process so if you going through deliverance, stick to it until you are totally delivered. The devil will send people from your past to cause you to fall or backslide. The devil will also intensify your temptations when you are seeking for deliverance. This is the reason why you have to read the Bible constantly and be in fellowship with mature Christians. Many times, people seeking for deliverance from demonic oppression are seriously attacked by the devil. This is the trick of the devil and his demons to discourage them from going ahead with the deliverance process. Once you become very determined and you persevere, they will release you. Sometimes, it gets worse before it gets better. Whatever the situation is, don't be discourage and don't give up. Jesus Christ will give you the victory you need. I strongly encourage people needing deliverance to be associated or connected to a

genuine Bible based deliverance ministries and also join a warfare prayer line.

Self-Deliverance Prayers

Luke 10 vs. 19 Prayers and confession for deliverance

The Lord will deliver me from every evil attack and bring me out safely into His heavenly kingdom to bring glory and honor to Jesus Christ my Lord and Savior.

Every evil covenant in my life with marine demons, spirit husband, spirit wife, witchcraft spirit, ancestral demons, be broken in my life by the blood of Jesus Christ.

Break now in my life in Jesus' name.

(Repeat 5x or more for all the prayers

Every Satanic powers, demonic powers, witchcraft powers, generational curses, and spells, afflicting and tormenting my body and my life be paralyzed and be bound in Jesus' name.

Release me in Jesus' name

You ancient strongman and demon enforcing evil curses in my life, I bind you in Jesus' name and I rebuke you by the blood of Jesus Christ

Every lips risen against me in judgment is destroyed in Jesus' name.

Let the fire of the Holy Ghost go into my body, soul, and spirit and break every covenants, yokes, chains, spell, and shackles from my life in Jesus name.

I drink the blood of Jesus Christ. Blood of Jesus Christ enter into my body, soul, and spirit and deliver me from every demonic oppression in Jesus' name

I command every demonic spirit out of my body in Jesus Mighty name. I bind you evil spirit and cast you out of my body and life. I do not have any covenant with you anymore because I have been redeemed by the blood of Jesus Christ.

I declare my liberty by faith in Jesus' name. I am free from demonic and witchcraft oppression in Jesus' name. Satan you are defeated in my life by the blood of Jesus Christ. I use the blood of Jesus Christ against you Satan and command your demons to leave my body and life in Jesus' name.

No weapon formed against me will ever prosper in Jesus' name.

I pull down every witchcraft alters in Jesus' name in my mother and fathers house.

I set every altars and family idols on fire in Jesus' name.

O God arise and scatter every powers of darkness contending against me in Jesus' name.

O God let your fire of deliverance deliver me from all my enemies in Jesus' name.

Read Galatians 3:13
Prayers

I am redeemed by the precious blood of Jesus Christ so my sins and the penalty of my sins have been forgiven because of the precious blood of Jesus.

There is therefore no condemnation against me because I am redeemed by the precious blood of Jesus Christ. I am redeemed from every generational curse because of the precious blood of Jesus Christ in Jesus' name.

I am redeemed from witchcraft initiation, influence, manipulations, control and dominion because I am redeemed by the precious blood of Jesus.

I break and nullify every curse I inherited through my blood line through conception, umbilical cord, birth canal and my mother's womb in Jesus' name.

I break myself loose and free from every generational spirit and curses by the precious blood of Jesus. I war with the blood of Jesus Christ to destroy every assignment of witchcraft against my life in Jesus' name. I break every generational marine witchcraft link in my life in Jesus' name.

Get a copy of my book "Freedom From Generational Curses and Strongholds." It will help you with self-deliverance and how to break generational curses.

Tips on Fasting

On Fresh Fire Prayer line, we fast twice a week. We fast on Tuesdays and Fridays and we meet in the evening for prayers. Fasting is very important in helping the Christian to grow spiritually. When you add fasting to your prayers, you get amazing results. Our motive for fasting twice a week is to draw closer to God and also to be spiritually sensitive to the Holy Spirit. During the fasting and prayer time, we spend more time in the word of God and prayers.

There are some stubborn problems that can only be dealt with through prayers and fasting. There are some powers of darkness which we can only overcome and overthrow through fasting and prayers.

We normally fast from 6am to 6pm. We drink only water during the fasting. After breaking the fast at 6pm, you can now eat. If you are not used to fasting, you are encouraged to start fasting from 6am to 12noon, 1pm, 2pm or 3pm until you get used to it. You can also fast by eating vegetables and fruits with water from 6am to 6pm. This is to get your body used to fasting thus if you are a beginner. This is to encourage beginners.

Whenever you have a very bad dream, you are advised to fast the next day to cancel it. When you have an interview, court case, exams, or need favor or deliverance, you are also advised to fast for favor and deliverance.

CHAPTER 5

Spiritual and Social History

SPIRITUAL HISTORY DEALS with your personal relationship with Jesus. Are you a Christian, have you backslidden as a Christian, or are you a lukewarm Christian? The Bible says, "Work out your salvation with fear and trembling." (Philippians 2:2)

It is possible to be very religious and yet not be a born again Christian. If you do not know Jesus as your Lord and personal Savior, then it is about time you gave your life to Jesus. Anyone who calls on the name of the Lord Jesus will be saved from his or her sins. Remember that every Christian and Pastor you see was once a sinner. We are all saved by the grace of God not by our righteous deeds. Jesus will forgive you of any sin. If you have backslidden or fallen from the faith then please slide back to God and get up from the floor of sin. God is a merciful Father and He will forgive you of all your sins like the prodigal son. God is well able to deliver you from every addiction that is holding you captive now. I pray now that the Spirit of God will set you loose and free from every addiction of sin that has ensnared you. May the spirit of God restore you back to your first love and your devotion to God. I see the Holy Spirit giving you power and divine strength to say NO to that sin and addiction. You are the righteousness of God, and sin and death do not have power of you. You are forgiven and free indeed. May the good Lord grant you the grace to join a Bible believing church to worship God.

Social history deals with the kind of friends we make and our lifestyle outside of church. The Bible says, **"Blessed is the man who walks not in the counsel of the ungodly, nor stands in the path of sinners, or sit in the seat of the scornful; but his delight is in the law of the LORD, and in His law he meditates day and night. He shall be like a tree planted by the rivers of water that brings forth its fruit in its season, whose leaf also shall not wither; and whatever he does shall prosper."** (Psalms 1:1-3)

"You are the light of the world. A city that is set on a hill cannot be hidden." (Matthew 5:14)

Jesus has placed a big responsibility on us as believers. He wants the world to see Him through us. The Hindu, Mahatma Gandhi, was moved to say: 'I love Christ, but I despise Christians because they do not live as Christ lived.' We need the Holy Spirit to give us the grace and strength to live as Christians. Without the power of the Holy Spirit working inside of us we can do nothing as believers. The Bible says, **"for it is God who is at work in you, both to will and to do his good pleasure."** (Philippians 2:13)

We need God to help us manifest the fruit of the Spirit. **"The fruit of the Spirit is love, joy, peace, patience, kindness, goodness, faithfulness, gentleness, and self-control. Against such things there is no law."** (Galatians 5:22-23)

"Though I speak with the tongues of men and angels, and have not love, I am become as sounding brass, or a tinkling cymbal. And though I have the gift of prophecy, and understand all mysteries, and all knowledge; and though I have faith, so that I could remove mountains, and have not love, I am nothing. And though I bestow all my goods to feed the poor, and though I give my body to be burned, and have not love, it profits me nothing. Love is patient, love is kind. It does not envy, it does not boast, it is not proud. It is not rude, it is not self-seeking, it is not easily angered, and it keeps no record of

wrongs. Love does not delight in evil but rejoices with the truth. It always protects, always trusts, always hopes, and always perseveres. Love never fails." (1 Corinthians 13:4-8)

We need the love of God in our lives in order to change the world.

CHAPTER 6

Spiritual Allergies and Assessment

ALLERGIES CAN BE defined as a strong dislike or aversion, as toward a person or activity. Spiritual allergies are a dislike towards good spiritual activities such as praying, fasting, bible studies, and church attendance. Some of us believers have an allergic reaction when it comes to praying. Any time we want to pray seriously we are easily distracted or we dose off. Some of us have allergic reaction towards bible studies. We don't have the discipline to do our own personal devotion. The bible seems to be a foreign language to us; we have no understanding when we read the bible. To others, fasting and all-night prayer services are out of the question. We love food too much to even sacrifice our breakfast for fasting and we are too busy to attend any all-night services. Some of us can stay at funeral services and parties for hours without complaining but one hour spent in the house of God is a problem. If we truly want to see the glory of God in our lives, then we have to overcome our spiritual allergies. We can do all things through Christ who strengthen us.

Spiritual assessment deals with evaluating our Christian life. The Bible says: **"For if we would judge ourselves, we should not be judged when we are judged by the Lord, we are being disciplined so that we will not be condemned with the world." (1 Corinthians 11: 31-32)**

Many of the trouble that we face in life are nothing more than God's way of judging us since we often neglect to judge ourselves. Would it not be great if every Christian actually took time to judge themselves before judging anyone else?

Personal Assessment

Am I truly a born-again believer or am I playing religion?

Do I have a personal relationship with Jesus?

I'm I dependent on God or Independent?

Do I read my Bible daily?

Do I rely on the Holy Spirit for guidance in my daily activities?

I'm I a fulltime Christian or a part-time Christian?

If God comes this very minute am I ready to be with Him?

Do I think about God and meditate on His words?

Do I spend time with God in prayers and worship?

Do I praising God or do I complain too much?

Do I really have faith in God?

Have I really surrendered my life to Jesus as my LORD and master?

Do I know the HOLY SPIRIT?

The First Step to Deliverance

The only true way for total and permanent deliverance from generational curses and strongholds is for one to become saved or born-again. To become a born-again Christian means to receive the Lord Jesus Christ into your heart and life as your Lord and personal savior.

Why you need to be Born-Again

The Bible declares, **"Therefore, just as through one man sin** entered the world, and death through sin, and thus death spread to all men, because all sinned." (Romans 5 vs. 12)

"For all have sinned and fall short of the glory of God." (Romans 3 vs. 23)

"As it is written: There is none righteous, no, not one." (Romans 3 vs. 10)

Above scriptures prove that we are all born sinful and none of us is innocent before God.

What is Sin?

Sin simply means missing God's mark or righteous standards. Sin is breaking of God's Law or commandments and rebelling or disobeying against God's will. The Bible says, **"Whoever commits sin also commits lawlessness, and sin is lawlessness."**

(1 John 3:14)

What Happens to Sinners?

The Bible declares, **"The soul who sins shall die." (Ezekiel 8:4).** **"For the wages of sin is death; but the gift of God is eternal life through Jesus Christ our Lord." (Romans 6:23).** These scriptures show that sinners will face the judgments of God.

How to become Saved/a Born-Again Christian

"For God so loved the world that He gave His only begotten Son, that whoever believes in Him should not perish but have everlasting life." (John 3 vs. 16)

"For whoever shall call upon the name of the Lord shall be saved." (Romans 10:13)

"Behold, now is the acceptable time; behold now is the day of salvation." (2 Colossians 6: 2)

To become saved or a born-again Christian, you have to believe in the Lord Jesus Christ, receive Him into your heart, and repent from all your sins. The Bible declares, **"If you confess with your mouth the Lord Jesus and believe in your heart that God has raised Him from the dead, you will be saved. For with the heart one believes unto righteousness, and with the mouth confession is made unto salvation. For the scriptures says, "Whoever believes on Him will not be put to shame." (Romans 9:9 - 12)**

Salvation Prayers

Heavenly Father, I ask for Your forgiveness for all my sins. I accept that I am a sinner and need Your Son Jesus Christ to forgive me from all my sins. I receive Jesus Christ into my heart as my Lord and personal savior today. I believe that Jesus Christ died for my sins and You raised Him up from the dead. Lord Jesus, I thank you for coming into my life. I give my body, soul, and spirit to You. Today, I put my trust in You Amen and amen.

If you prayed this prayer sincerely from your heart, then you are now a born-again Christian. Only believe and the Holy Spirit will help you and lead you into all truth in the Bible. You are now a new creature. The Bible says, **"Therefore, if anyone is in Christ, he is a new creature; old things have passed away; behold all things have become new." (2 Corinthians 5 vs. 17)**

You are now ready to enjoy all the benefits of salvation through the precious blood of Jesus Christ.

Some benefits of salvation: Deliverance, joy, peace, good health, prosperity, liberty, favor, blessing, etc.

CHAPTER 7

Weapons of War

IT IS WRITTEN, **"For the weapons of our warfare are not carnal but mighty in God for pulling down strongholds, casting down arguments and every high thing that exalts itself against the knowledge of God, bringing every thought into captivity to the obedience of Christ, and being ready to punish all disobedience when your obedience is fulfilled." (2 Corinthian 10: 4-6)**

The Name of Jesus

"The name of the Lord is a strong tower: the righteous runneth into it, and is safe." (Proverbs 18: 10)

"Therefore God also has highly exalted Him (Jesus) and given Him the name which is above every name, that at the name of Jesus every knee should bow, of those in heaven, and of those on earth, and of those under the earth, and that every tongue should confess that Jesus Christ is Lord, to the glory of God the Father." (Philippians 2:9-11)

Principalities, powers, rulers of the darkness of this world, spiritual hosts of wickedness in the heavenly places, demons, witchcraft, family idols and voodoo are all rendered powerless, weak and impotent at the mention of the name Jesus in faith. When the name of Jesus is mentioned in faith, every knee bows things on earth, things underneath the earth, and things in heaven. When you use the name of Jesus in your prayers all wicked spirit fighting you begin to run away.

Satan and his cohorts are afraid of the name of Jesus. When the names of Jesus is used in faith in prayers against any problem, the demons and the agents of the evil behind the problem lose control and are cast out. In the name of Jesus, there is power, healing, and deliverance. The name of Jesus is a **spiritual atomic bomb** that gets stubborn problems solved. It is not just a religious title we mention at the end of our prayers. God hears our prayer because of the name of Jesus and demons flee from us because of the name of Jesus.

"And these signs shall follow them that believe; in my name (Jesus) they shall cast out devils; they shall speak with new tongues." (Mark 16:17)

My friend, don't toy with the name of Jesus. **It is the most valuable weapon you have in your hands to frustrate, disgrace, and humiliate the works of the devil in your life.** The name of Jesus is an unchallengeable weapon against cancer, tumor, death and any evil plot of Satan against you and your family. Don't allow the devil to steal, kill and destroy your job, family, health, finances, and marriage when you have this great atomic bomb in Jesus name available to you to destroy the works of Satan concerning your life. I dare you to begin to use the name of Jesus in faith in your prayers against every problem and you will see results. The Bible says that anything we ask from the Lord God in prayers must be done in the name and authority of the Lord Jesus Christ.

"And whatsoever ye shall ask in my name, that will I do, that the Father may be glorified in the Son."(John 14:13)

"And in that day ye shall ask me nothing. Verily, verily, I say unto you, whatsoever ye shall ask the Father in my name, he will give it to you. Hitherto have ye asked nothing in my name: ask, and ye shall receive, that your joy may be full. At that day ye shall ask in my

name; and I say not unto you, that I will pray the Father for you." (John 16:23, 24, 26)

"And whatsoever ye do in word or deed, do all in the name of the Lord Jesus, giving thanks to God and the Father by him." (Colossians 3:17)

"Then Peter said, Silver and gold have I none; but such as I have I give thee: In the name of Jesus Christ of Nazareth rise up and walk." (Act 3:6)

"Let it be known unto you all, and to all the people of Israel, that by the name of Jesus Christ of Nazareth, whom ye crucified, whom God raised from the dead, even by Him doth this man stand here before you whole."(Act 4:10)

Every child of God who has received Jesus Christ as their Lord and personal savior is entitled to use the name of Jesus for great results. Jesus said, **"most assuredly, I say to you, he who believes in Me, the works that I do he will do also; and greater works than these he will do, because I go to My Father. And whatever you ask in My name, that I will do, that the Father may be glorified in the Son. If you ask anything in My name, I will do it." (John 14:12-14)**

"Neither is there salvation in any other name, for there is no other name under heaven given among men, whereby we must be saved." (Act 4:12)

May the name of Jesus save you from the snare of the fowler, and from the perilous pestilence. May the name of Jesus save you from the terror by night and the arrows of the devil that flies by day. May the name of Jesus protect you and your family from the destruction that lays waste at noonday. May a thousand fall at your side and ten thousand at your right hand because of the name of Jesus.

Song about the name Jesus:

When troubles surround me
I did not have to despair
The Lord did told me that He would always be there

Seems like all my problems they just began
But I didn't have to worry because they have already been won
Oh, Jesus, my sweet Jesus
How I love calling your name.
Everyday your name is the same.

The Blood of Jesus

"And they overcame him by the blood of the lamb..." (Revelation 12:11a)

Whenever the blood of Jesus is used in warfare it destroys the works of the enemy. Satan and his agents cannot penetrate the blood of Jesus to touch the children of God. When the blood is invoked in faith and with meaning it erases every Satanic plans, programs, prediction, projections and expectations against the child of God. The blood of Jesus brings liberty, freedom, and emancipation to anyone who is bound in sin, chains and shackles of the devil. The blood of Jesus is another spiritual atomic bomb which when released scatters the devil and his cohorts. **Satan cannot simply stand the power of the blood of Jesus. The blood of Jesus serves as our Passover.**

"And the blood shall be to you for a token upon the houses where ye are: and when I see the blood. I will pass over you, and the plaque shall not be upon you to destroy you, when I smite the land of Egypt."(Exodus 12:13)

"Therefore purge out the old leaven, that you may be a new lump, since you truly are unleavened. For indeed Christ, our Passover was sacrificed for us." (Corinthians 5:7)

The angel of death could not touch the children of Israel because of the blood of a lamb, which they used on their doorpost. **When the angel of death saw the blood he passed over the children of Israel.** However, with the Egyptians they were killed by the angel of death because they had no protection. **The blood of Jesus is an impregnable wall of protection for every child of God redeem by Jesus.** If you are a Christian you are entitled to use the blood of Jesus in your prayers for protection against the devil. You can immerse yourself in the blood of Jesus, your children, your properties in the blood Jesus. It will serve as divine protection from the enemy. When the devil and his cohorts see the blood of Jesus on you and your family **they will Passover you**. Sickness, accidents, and Satanic operations targeted against you when they see the blood they will Passover you because of the blood of Jesus. May the blood of Jesus protect your body from sickness and Satanic implantations, May the blood of Jesus protect your children, and cars from accident. May the blood of Jesus protect you from every spell and curse issued against you by any powers of darkness and may you overcome your enemies by the blood of the lamb of Jesus.

The Angels of God

"Are they not all ministering spirits sent forth to minister for those who will inherit salvation?" (Hebrews 1:!4)

"The angel of the Lord encampeth round about them that fear Him, and delivereth them." (Psalm 34:7)

Angels do minister to believers. The guardian angels of the children of God are beholding the face of God continually. (Matthew 18 vs. 10) You are not alone. It is about time you tell your heavenly Father to deploy his angel to assist you and protect you from the traps of the enemy. It is about time you employ the services of heaven to deploy angel to fight your battles. The angels are waiting to serve you just ask the Father in Jesus name and he will send them to help you. The Bible declares, **"now because of this King Hezekiah and the prophet Isaiah, the son of Amoz, prayed and cried out to heaven, Then the LORD sent an angel who cut down every mighty man of valor, leader, and captain in the camp of the king of Assyria. So he returned shamefaced to his own land. And when he had gone into the temple of his god, some of his own offspring struck him down with the word there. Thus the LORD saved Hezekiah and the inhabitants of Jerusalem from the hand of Sennacherib the King of Assyria,** and from the hand of all others, and guided them on every side." (2 Chronicles 32:20-22)

"And it came to pass that night, that the angel of the Lord went out, and smote in the camp of the Assyrians an hundred four score and five thousand; and when they arose early in the morning, behold these were all dead corpses." (2 Kings 19:35)

This is what I am talking about! Devine protection from the enemy. The King of Assyria was bent on invading Jerusalem to take it for himself and make slaves off the children of God. He was a great King and had won many battles against stronger nations. Israel was no match for him at all. When the King of Israel released that all hope was gone, he handed the battle to the lord with prayers. And the LORD God deployed his mighty angels to take care of business for the children of God. At night the angel of the lord went to the camp of the Assyrians and killed the soldiers. The Israelite did have to fight. The angel of the lord took care of business for them. It is high time you stop fighting your own battles. Let God deploy or send his angels to take care of your enemies for you. The angel of the Lord will deliver you from the traps of your enemies if you employ their services from God in Jesus name. Daniel said to King Darius, "my God hath sent His angels, and have shut the lions' mouth, that they have not hurt me." (Daniel 6:22)

Peter was delivered from prison by God's mighty angels. But first the disciples were praying to God for him. They employed the services of heaven and God sent down his angel to deliver Peter from prison.

"Peter therefore was kept in prison: but prayers were made without ceasing of the church for unto God for him. And when Herod would have brought him forth, the same night Peter was sleeping between two soldiers, bound with two chains: and the keepers before the door kept the prison: And behold, the angel of the Lord came upon him, and a light shined in the prison: and he smote Peter on the side, and raised him up, saying, Arise up quickly. And his chains fell off from his hands." (Act 12:5-7)

May the Lord give His angel charge over you, to keep you in all your ways. In their hand they shall bear you up, lest you dash your foot against a stone. May the angel of the Lord chase and persecute your enemies. May your enemies' way be dark and slippery and let them be like chaff before the wind. Let your enemies who seek after you life be put to shame and brought to dishonor. Let them be turned back and brought to confusion who plot your hurt in Jesus name.

The Word of God

"In the beginning was the Word, and the Word was with God, and the Word was God. He was in the beginning with God. All things were made through Him, and without Him nothing was made that was made. In Him was life, and the life was the light of men. And the light shines in the darkness, and the darkness did not comprehend it." (John 1-3)

Jesus Christ is the Word of God. The Word of God is more powerful than atomic bomb, and when used in faith, one is guaranteed great results. We have to have an unflinching belief in the Word of God. The Bible declares, **"For You (God) have magnified Your word above all Your name."** (Psalm 138:2)

Satan cannot stand the word of God. That is the reason why Jesus Christ used the word of God to defeat Satan when He was tempted after the forty days fasting. All Jesus did was to quote the relevant scriptures to defeat the devil. The devil does not argue when you use the scriptures against him. Demons feel uncomfortable when the word of God is used against them. Find the scriptural fact about every problem you are facing and apply the word in faith against the problem and the problem will melt away.

Mixing the Word of God with Faith

"It is the spirit that quickeneth; the flesh profiteth nothing: the words that I speak unto you, they are spirit, and they are life." (John 6:63)

"He sent his word, and healed them, and delivered them from their destructions." (Psalm 107:20)

"And it came to pass on a certain day, as he was teaching (Word), that there were Pharisees and doctors of the law sitting by, which were come out of every town of Galilee, and Judea, and Jerusalem: and the power of the Lord was present to heal them." (Luke 5:17)

"For there are three that bear record in heaven, the Father, the Word, and the Holy Ghost: and these three are one." (1 John 5:7)

"For the word of God is living and powerful, and sharper than any two-edged sword, piercing even to the division of soul and spirit, and of joints and marrow, and is discerner of the thoughts and intents of the heart." (Hebrews 4:12)

"Is not my word like a fire? Saith the Lord; and like a hammer that breaketh the rock in pieces?" (Jeremiah 23:29)

God's Word is as fire and it will melt down every problem in your life. God's Word is a hammer that will break every mountain confronting you into pieces. Your problems are not moved by your tears and sadness; they are only moved by the word of God. Whatever problem you are facing locates the relevant scripture that deals with the problem and apply the word of God in faith and you will see wonderful results. The Bible says, "**But the just shall live by his faith.**" **(Habakkuk 2:4b)**

"**But without faith it is impossible to please Him (God),** for he who comes to God must believe that He is, and that He is a rewarder of those who diligently seek Him." (Hebrews 11 vs. 6)

"**By faith we understand that the worlds were framed by the word of God,** so that the things which are seen were not made of things which are visible." (Hebrews 11 vs. 3)

"By faith Sarah herself also received strength to conceive a seed, and she bore a child when she was past the age, because she judged Him faithful who had promised." (Hebrews 11: 11)

"Who against hope believed in hope, that he might become the father of many nations, according to that which was spoken, so shall they seed be. **And being not weak in faith,** he considered not his own body now dead, when he was about a hundred years old, neither yet the deadness of Sarah's womb: **He staggered not at the promise of God through unbelief; but was strong in faith, giving glory to God; And being fully persuaded that, what he (God) had promised, he was able to perform."** (Romans 4:18-21)

"For indeed the gospel was preached to us as well as them; **but the word which they heard did not profit them, not being mixed with faith in those who heard it."** (Hebrews 4:2)

"Now faith is the substance of things hoped for, the evidence of things not seen." (Hebrews 11: 1)

"But they have not all obeyed the gospel. For Isaiah says, "LORD, **who has believe our report?" So then faith comes by hearing, and hearing by the word of God."** (Romans 10:17)

"And what more shall I say? For the time would fail me to tell of Gideon and Barak and Samson and Jephthah, also of David and Samuel and the prophets: who through faith subdued kingdoms, worked righteousness, obtained promises, stopped the mouths of lions, quenched the violence of fire, escaped the edge of the sword, out of weakness were made strong, became valiant in battle, turned to flight the armies of aliens. Women received their dead raised to life again." (Hebrews 11:32-35).

It is not how many times we pray and how long we pray to God that matters, it is all about the faith behind the prayers that brings about tremendous results. Prayers without faith do not get any re-sults. Why do some Christians see daily miracles in their lives while other believers have dry experience with God? The answer to this question is because of lack of faith. Many genuine believers suffer from a sickness called '**Thomas syndrome'. Thomas syndrome is characterized by the spirit of doubt, unbelief and skepticism**. Christians diagnosed with Thomas syndrome do not see the miraculous, signs and wonders of God in their lives. They doubt the word of God, the speaking in tongues, angels, the move of the spirit, prophesies, the existence of Satan and his cohorts. They are worse of than people who are unbelievers and have never received Jesus as their Lord and personal savior. Yet they can be very religious and very active in the church. Christians who have Thomas syndrome kill church growth and the move of the spirit in the church. They are satisfied with religion and have settled down and become stationary and stagnant Christians. They have no vision so they are constantly using their carnal mind to judge the things of the spirit. They ignorantly fight the work of God because of lack of spiritual understanding due to unbelief. They are good people but are tools used by devil to destroy the work of God in the body of Christ. We need to cast out the spirit of unbelief, doubt, religion, and skepticism from the Church of God and set people free from Thomas syndrome. If we do this, people will be receptive to the gospel of our Lord Jesus and we will see the glory of God in our churches.

"Now it came to pas, when Jesus had finished these parables that He departed from there. When He had come to His own country, He taught them in their synagogue, so that they were astonished and said, " where did this Man get this wisdom and these mighty works? Is this not the carpenter's son? Is not His mother called Mary? And His brothers James, Joses, Simon, and Judas? And His sisters, are they not all with us? Where then did this Man get all these things? **So they were offended at Him.** But Jesus said to them, "A prophet is not without honor except in his own country and in his own house. **Now He did not do many mighty works there because of their unbelief."** **(Matthews 13:53-57)**

"Death and life are in the power of the tongue, and those who love it will eat its fruits." (Proverbs 18:21)

"Then the hand of the LORD came upon me and brought me out in the Spirit of the LORD, and set me down in the midst of the valley; and it was full of bones. Then He caused me to pass by them all around, and behold, there were very many in the open valley; and indeed they were very dry. And He said to me, "Son of man, can these bones live? So I answered, "O Lord GOD, You know." Again He said to me, "Prophesy to these bones, and say to them, ' O dry bones, hear the word of the LORD! Thus says the Lord God to these bones: Surely I will cause breath to enter into you, and you shall live. I will put sinews on you and bring flesh upon you, cover you with skin and put breath in you; and you shall live. Then you shall know that I am the LORD." So I prophesied as I was commanded; and as I prophesied, there was a noise, and suddenly a rattling; and the bones came together, bone to bone. Indeed, as I looked, the sinews and the flesh came upon them, and the skin covered them over..." (Ezekiel 37:1-8)

God is asking you whether you believe that your dry marriage can come back to live, your dry bank account can come back to live, your dry relationship with your children can come back to life, your dry womb can come back to live, your dry health can come back to live. God says, "Son of man do you believe." If you don't know how God is going to do the impossible, reverse the irreversible and change the unchangeable don't doubt His ability just say to Him 'LORD only you know'. God is asking you right now by faith to prophesy to your dead and dry situation and the Holy Ghost will begin to bring things back to life in Jesus name.

You become what you confess. I dare you to confess these declarations **in faith in Jesus' name**.

It shall be well with me in Jesus' name.

The purpose of God for my life shall be fulfilled in Jesus' name.

I will not fail in life in Jesus' name.

It shall be well with me and my family in Jesus' name.

Every mountain in my life shall be moved in Jesus' name.

Anyone blocking my way shall become a stepping-stone to my testimony in Jesus' name.

I will reach the top this year in Jesus' name.

Every good thing that I need, the Almighty God will send it to me in Jesus' name.

Wherever my help may be, God will send it to me in Jesus' name.

Anyone sitting on my promotion, God shall set fire on their buttocks in Jesus' name.

Through me, God will be glorified in Jesus' name.

Sorrow shall become a stranger to me in Jesus' name.

God Almighty will enlarge my coast this year in Jesus' name.

God will prosper me this year in Jesus' name.

I will get married in Jesus' name.

I will have my children in Jesus' name.

Something good, glorious, wonderful, beautiful, and great will happen to me this year in Jesus' name.

I refuse to be denied, delayed, rejected, disappointed, and disgraced in Jesus' name.

I shall not be moved by what I see, hear, and by any problems in Jesus' name.

I shall not be moved by the doctors and lawyers bad report in Jesus' name.

I shall not be moved by my debt, creditors, and any financial crisis in Jesus' name.

I shall not be moved by marital problems, stubborn children, and barrenness in Jesus name.

I am blessed and highly favored in Jesus' name.

I am blessed and not cursed in Jesus' name.

I receive financial assistance from heaven above in Jesus' name.

I receive my breakthrough this year in Jesus' name.

I receive my children in Jesus' name.

I receive a good marriage in Jesus' name.

I receive my life's partner in Jesus' name.

I receive a good job in Jesus' name.

I receive my healing and deliverance in Jesus' name.

I receive restoration of my marriage and family in Jesus' name.

I receive anointing and favor for exploit in Jesus' name.

I shall be the head and not the tail in Jesus' name.

All things whether good, bad, or ugly will work for my good in Jesus' name.

I shall not die but live and declare the wonderful works of the Lord in Jesus' name.

Testimonies

"And they overcame him (Satan) by the blood of the Lamb and by the word of their testimony; and they loved not their lives unto the death." (Revelations 12:11)

It is time we stop complaining about our problems and trials and begin to give testimonies about the goodness of the lord in our lives. If you are alive then you have a testimony. Count your blessings and testify about the faithfulness of God. **The Bible says that it is of the Lord's mercies that we are not consumed because His compassion do not fail they are new every morning and great is God's faithfulness**

towards us. When you testify about the goodness of God in your life concerning little things you provoke God to do even much greater things in your life.

Stop narrating stories of woe to every body you come into contact with and begin to glorify God and encourage other believers with your testimony. It will surprise you to know that somebody in another continent desires so badly to have just a fraction of what you have. Don't let your problems overwhelm you to the extent that you lose sight of God blessings in your life. Remember that once there is life then there is hope and no condition is permanent. Find relevant testimonies in your life, and wrap them in the blood and begin to glorify God and encourage other brethren with it. **The more you testify of God's goodness and faithfulness in your life, the more you will receive victory over your problems and open doors in your life.** David used the word of testimony to build his faith and confidence in God and he was able to defeat Goliath and collect his head. The Bible declares, **"and Saul said to David, You are not able to go against this Philistine to fight with him; for you are a youth, and he a man of war from his youth." But David said to Saul, "Your servant used to keep his father's sheep, and when a lion or a bear came and took a lamb out of the flock, I went out after it and struck it, and delivered the lamb from its mouth; and when it arose against me, I caught it by its beard, and struck and killed it. Your servant has killed both lion and bear; and this uncircumcised Philistine will be like one of them, seeing he has defied the armies of the living God." Moreover David said, "The LORD, who delivered me from the paw of the lion and from the paw of the bear, He will deliver me from the hand of this Philistine."** And Saul said to David, "Go, and the LORD be with you!" (1 Samuel 17:33-37)

"Then David said to the Philistine, **"You come to me with a sword, with a spear, and with a javelin. But I come to you in the name of the LORD of hosts, the God of the armies of Israel, whom you have defied. This day the LORD will deliver you into my hands, and I will** strike you and take your head from you. And this day I will give the carcasses of the camp of the Philistines to the birds of the air and the wild beasts of the earth, that all the earth may know that there is a God in Israel. Then all this assembly shall know that the LORD does not save with sword and spear; for the battle is the LORD's and He will give you into our hands."

My question to you is where is your testimony to defeat your Goliath?

Praise and Worship

Praise and worship is another powerful weapon against Satan and his cohorts. In the face of any difficulty when you begin to praise and worship God, God comes down to fight for you. Wherever God is there is absolute victory over Satan and his demons. **God inhabit the praise of his people.** Inhabit means to dwell in or live in or abide in. God lives in our praise. The Bible declares, **"But You (God) are holy, Enthroned in the praises of Israel." (Psalm 22:3)**

The Israelites use praise to pull down the strong wall of Jericho. Paul and Silas were visited by the power of God when they prayed and praised God in hymns in their prison cell.

"And when they had laid many stripes on them (Paul and Silas), they threw them into prison, commanding the jailer to keep them securely. Having received such a charge, he put them into the inner prison and fastened their feet in the stocks. But at midnight Paul and Silas were praying and singing hymns to God, and the prisoners were listening to them. Suddenly there was a great earthquake, so that the foundations of the prison were shaken; and immediately all the doors were opened and everyone's chains were loosed." (Acts 16:23-26)

When we begin to praise and worship God, Satanic chains, shackles and padlocks begin to break by the power of God. People in any form of bondage and cage are delivered from the grips of the devil and his cohort. We don't have to praise God only in good times. We have to learn to praise and worship God at all times. **We have to praise and worship God in good times, bad times and the ugly moments in our lives.** When you begin to praise and worship God in the face of trials and tribulations, negative mood such as depression and anxiety begin to disappear. The presence of God drives out emotional pain and the spirit of fear, discouragement and hopelessness gives way to the peace and joy of the Holy Ghost. When we praise and worship God, God becomes bigger than our problems and our problems melt before us at the presence of God in our worship. Praise and worship are great medicine to the soul and it heals all emotional pains. The Bible declares, **"I will bless the LORD at all times; His praise shall continually be in my mouth. My soul shall make its boast in the LORD; The humble shall hear of it and be glad. Oh, magnify the LORD with me, And let us exalt His name together." (Psalms 34:1-3)**

"Bless the LORD, O my soul; And all that is within me, bless His holy name! Bless the LORD, O my soul, and forget not all His benefits: Who forgives all your iniquities, Who heals all your diseases, Who redeems your life from destruction, Who crowns you with loving kindness and tender mercies, Who satisfies your mouth with good things, So that your youth is renewed like the eagle's." (Psalm 103:1-5)

"You have turned for me my mourning into dancing; You have put off my sackcloth and clothed me with gladness, To the end that my glory may sing praise to You and not be silent. O LORD my God, I will give thanks to You forever." (Psalm 30:11-12)

"Praise the LORD! Praise God in His sanctuary; Praise Him in His mighty firmament! Praise Him for His mighty acts; Praise Him according to His excellent greatness! Praise Him with the sound of the trumpet; Praise Him with the lute and harp! Praise Him with the timbre and dance, Praise Him with stringed instruments and flutes! Praise Him with loud cymbals; Praise Him with clashing cymbals!

Let everything that has breath praise the LORD. Praise the LORD!"

The Fire of God

It is important for you to understand that Jehovah God is a consuming fire. The Bible says, **"For the Lord thy God is a consuming fire, even a jealous God." (Deuteronomy 4:24)**

"For our God is a consuming fire."(Hebrews 12:29)

Whenever God moves his consuming fire goes ahead of him to destroy his enemies. Whenever you invite God to fight for you concerning any problem, His fire melts down any problems you present to him.

"Behold, I am the LORD, the God of all flesh: is there anything too hard for me?" (Jeremiah 32:37)

Whenever you invoke the judgment fire of God against your enemies in your prayers, you are sure of total victory over them. The fire of God will consume all their evil plans and programs concerning you. When you invoke the judgment fire of God in warfare prayers, every Satanic altar erected for your destruction is burnt down into ashes. When the consuming fire of God is directed at the cabinet meeting place of your enemies, it suffocates the witches and wizards and scatters them. The fire of God when applied correctly in faith is a deadly weapon in the hands of the believer. Satan and his cohorts cannot stand the heat generated by the fire of God. Every problem melts like wax at the presence of God's fire. The Bible declares, **"A fire goes before him, and burns up his enemies round about. His lightning's enlightened the world: the earth saw, and trembled. The hills melted like wax at the presence of the LORD, at the presence of the Lord of the whole earth." (Psalm 97: 3-5)**

"Our God shall come, and shall not keep silence: a fire shall devour before him, and it shall be very tempestuous round about him." (Psalm 50:3)

"And the LORD said, because the cry of Sodom and Gomorrah

is great, and because their sin is very grievous..." (Genesis 18:20)

"Then the Lord rained upon Sodom and upon Gomorrah brimstone and fire from the LORD out of heaven; and he overthrew those cities, and all the plain, and all the inhabitants of the cities, and that which grew upon the ground." (Genesis 19:24-25)

"And when the people complained, it displeased the LORD: and the LORD heard it, and his anger was kindled; and the fire of the LORD burnt among them, and consumed them that were in the uttermost parts of the camp. And the people cried unto Moses; and when Moses prayed unto the LORD, the fire was quenched." (Numbers 11:1-2)

It must be noted here that the judgment fire of God is not only a lethal weapon against the devil and his agents outside the church, but it is also an instrument of judgment against the spirit of wickedness, rebellion, disobedience and confusion in the house of God.

Elijah knew just how to use the judgment fire of God to deal with his enemies. When King Ahaziah the son of Ahab and Jezebel sent two groups of fifty soldiers to have Elijah arrested, Elijah used the judgment fire of God to defeat them. The Bible says:

"Then the king sent to him a captain of fifty with his fifty men. So he went up to him; and there he was, sitting on the top of a hill. And he spoke to him: **"Man of God, the king has said, come down!"** So Elijah answered and said to the captain of fifty, **'If I am a man of God, then let fire come down from heaven and consume you and your fifty men." And fire came down from heaven and consumed him and his fifty.** Then he sent him another captain of fifty with his fifty men. And he answered and said to him, **"man of God thus has the king said, 'Come down quickly!'" So Elijah answered and said to them, "If I am a man of God, let fire come down from heaven and consume you and your fifty men." And the fire of God came down from heaven and consumed him and his fifty."** (2 Kings 1:9-12) You can also pray similar prayers in faith and get similar results. The Bible says Elijah was a man with like passions like us. You can pray like this:

If I be a child of God, then let fire come down from heaven and burn into ashes every Satanic agents working against my success, promotion, prosperity, breakthrough, goals, vision, dreams, happiness, joy, and peace in Jesus' name.

If I be a child of God, then let fire come down from heaven and consume into ashes every Satanic padlocks, chains, shackles, roadblocks, and obstacles put in place to prevent me from achieving my goals and dreams in life in Jesus' name.

If I be a child of God, then let fire come down from heaven and consume into ashes every evil plans, programs, expectations, prediction and projection against my health, finances, marriage, family, children, and Job in Jesus' name.

If I be a child of God, then let fire come down from heaven and consume into ashes every evil altar erected for my destruction, every false prophet pronouncing curses on me and my family, every divination, incantation, and charm against me and my family, every agent monitoring my progress in life. Let them receive the judgment fire of God in Jesus' name.

The fire of God also protects us from our enemies. The Bible says that after the King of Syria found out that Elisha the prophet was the one who was leaking his plans against Israel to the King of Israel, the King of Syria decided to have him arrested and killed by his great army. He knew that if he could get rid of Elisha then it will be easy for him defeat the nation of Israel. The Bible declares, "Therefore, the heart of the king of Syria was greatly troubled by this thing; and he called his servants and said to them, "Will you not show me which of us is for the king of Israel?" And one of his servants said, "None my Lord, O king; but Elisha, the prophet who is in Israel, tells the king of Israel the words that you speak in your bedroom." So he said, "Go and see where he is, that I may send and get him."

And it was told him, saying, "Surely he is in Dothan." Therefore he sent horses and chariots and a great army there, and they came by the night and surrounded the city. And when the servant of the man of God arose early and went out, there was an army, surrounding the city with horses and chariots. And his servant said to him, "Alas, my master! What shall we do?" So he (Elisha) answered, **Do not fear, for those who are with us are more than those who are with them."** And Elisha prayed, and said, **LORD, I pray, open his eyes that he may see." Then the LORD opened the eyes of the young man, and he saw. And behold, the mountain was full of horses and chariots of fire all around Elisha." (2 Kings 6:11-17)**

As a child of God, don't be intimidated by evil forces against you because you are never alone. Invoke divine protection on your life. Tell your heavenly father to protect you and your family with horses and chariots of fire round about in Jesus' name.

It is important for us to understand that until you are a born-again believer, you do not have access to these lethal weapons mentioned above. These weapons of warfare are for children of the kingdom. The Bible says that unto the children of God only is it given to know the mysteries of the kingdom of God. Unto others, they are parables. They can only be used by people who have received Jesus as their Lord and personal savior and are filled with the Holy Ghost power. It must also be noted here that part-time Christians will not see the effectiveness of these weapons of warfare. They are deadly and effective weapons in the hands of full-time Christians; people who have dedicated their life fully to follow Jesus. This is what happens if you are not a child of God and you try to use these lethal weapons against the devil and his cohorts. The Bible declares: "Now God worked unusual miracles by the hands of Paul, so that even handkerchiefs or aprons were brought from his body to the sick, and the disease left them and the evil spirit went out of them. Some of the itinerant Jewish exorcists took it upon themselves to call the name of the Lord over those who had evil spirits, saying, "We exorcise you by the Jesus whom Paul preaches." Also there were seven sons of Sceva, a Jewish chief priest, who did so. **And the evil spirit answered and said, "Jesus I know, and Paul I know; but who are you?" Then the**

man in whom the evil spirit was leaped on them, overpowered them, and prevailed against them, so that they fled out of that house naked and wounded." (Acts 19:11-16)

Other Weapons of Warfare

The arm of the Lord: (Isaiah 51 vs. 9)

Fishers and Hunters of God: (Jeremiah 16 vs. 16-17)

The voice of the Lord: (Psalm 29 vs. 3-9)

East wind of God: (Jeremiah 18 vs.17)

Horses and Chariot of fire: (2 king 6 vs.17), (Isaiah 66 vs. 15-16)

The angel of God: (Exodus 23 vs. 20), (2 Chronicles 32 vs. 21)

Hail stones: (Joshua 10 vs. 10)

Thunder: (1 Samuel 2 vs. 10)

Lightning, arrows, and scattering: (Psalm 144)

Shame, dishonor, confusion, and unexpected destruction: (Psalm 35 vs. 1-8)

God fighting for you: (Exodus 14 vs. 14)

The Full Armor of God

"Therefore take up the whole armor of God that you may be able to withstand in the evil day, and having done all, to stand. Stand therefore, having girded your waist with truth, having put on the breast plate of righteousness, and having shod your feet with the preparation of the gospel of peace; above all, take the shield of faith with which you will be able to quench all the fiery darts of the wicked one. And the helmet of salvation, and the sword of the Spirit, which is the word of God." (Ephesians 6:13-17)

To effectively win the battle against the enemy, you have to make sure that you are putting on the full armor of God. Failure to put

on the full armor of God will render us vulnerable to our enemies' attacks.

Your waist with truth: Jesus is the way, truth and life. The Bible says that God should sanctify us by His word for His word is truth. Jesus Christ is the word of God and He is truth. We have to build our foundation in life on Jesus Christ and His written commandment in the Bible.

Breast plate of righteousness: The breast plate protects the vital organs like the heart. The Bible says that out of the heart comes the issues of life and a man's heart is deceitful above all things who can know it. For us to win the battle against our enemies, we have to be holy and righteous. We have to protect our heart from all contamination, filthiness, and pollutions of sin.

Feet with the preparation of the gospel of peace: As believers, it is our duty to go out into the world and spread the gospel of our Lord Jesus Christ to unbelievers. We have to depopulate hell and populate heaven by telling people about Jesus Christ and asking people to receive Him into their lives us their Lord and personal savior.

Shield of faith: Without faith, it is impossible to please God. Faith comes by hearing and hearing the word of God. If you have faith in God, you can move every mountain and overcome every enemy in Jesus' name.

Helmet of salvation: We always have to make sure we are in the faith. The Bible says that with fear and trembling we should work out our own salvation. We have to make sure we are living a holy and righteous life and worshipping God in truth and in spirit.

CHAPTER 8

Spiritual Tips

1. Make sure you are in good standing with God. Confess your sins, repent from your sins, and forsake your sins.

2. Have faith in God. All things are possible with God and to them that believe in God.

3. **Learn to say 'it is well' no matter what problems may come your way.**

4. Learn to praise God when the going gets tough.

5. **Look at the bright side of things.**

6. Learn to encourage yourself in the Lord.

7. **Pray the prayer of Jabez at least once a week.**

8. Introduce Psalms 35 and 91 into your prayers.

9. **Ask the lord to show you His mercy, grace, and favor.**

10. Use the blood of Jesus to destroy the works of the devil.

11. **Immerse yourself and your family in the blood of Jesus for divine protection.**

12. Ask God to send His angel to watch over you and your family.

13. **Use the name of Jesus to destroy the activities of Satan.**

14. Build your spirit man with the word of God, fasting and prayers.

15. **Pray in your heavenly language (Tongues)**

16. Don't sit down for any problem to kill you seek for help.

17. **Don't just accept every negative prophecies from a prophet, reverse them in Jesus' name.**

18. There are levels of anointing in breaking yokes and curses. Combine your anointing with someone more anointed than you to deal with your stubborn problem.

19. **Don't play with your prayer life. A prayerless Christian is a powerless Christian.**

20. Take responsibility for your own problems your pastor can only help but your aggressiveness in the spirit and your faith will give you the victory.

21. **Have faith, pray and be in expectation to receive from God.**

22. Don't wait till the church calls for a fast before you fast. Fast and pray to receive strength from God to overcome your problems.

23. **After you've done all you can just be still and wait for God to do His job.**

CHAPTER 9

Strategic Prayer Points

1. Lord, bless me and bless me indeed in Jesus' name.

2. Lord, bless me with your favor, goodness, grace, and mercy in Jesus' name.

3. Lord, bless me with your peace, joy, and understanding in my marriage in Jesus' name.

4. Lord, bless me with good health and long life in Jesus' name.

5. Lord, bless me with your anointing, wisdom, and your presence in Jesus' name.

6. Lord, enlarge my territory and stretch the limitations of my boundaries in Jesus' name.

7. Lord, enlarge my coast; let me launch deep into your blessings in Jesus' name.

8. Lord, roll away my reproach, shame, disappointment, and failure from my life in Jesus' name.

9. Lord, bless me to be a blessing.

10. Lord let me know you and the power of your resurrection.

11. Let God arise and my enemies be scattered.

12. Lord, do a new thing in my life. Turn my defeat to victory, my shame to glory, my weeping to laughter, and put a new song

in my mouth.

13. Heavenly Father, send help from the east, west, north, and south. Send help from heaven above.

14. Lord let the heavens above me be opened.

15. Lord turn the table against my enemies.

16. Let every Satanic agenda for my destiny be destroyed in Jesus' name.

17. Every evil power that pursued my parents be destroyed, in the name of Jesus.

18. Negative inheritance from my family, die, in the name of Jesus.

19. Fire of God, separate me from my inherited darkness, in the name of Jesus.

20. Let the confidence of the wicked be broken, in the name of Jesus.

21. I reject every Satanic re-arrangement of my destiny, in Jesus' name.

22. Holy Ghost power, uproot every wicked implantation from my life, in Jesus' name.

23. O' God arise and uproot anything you did not plant inside me, in Jesus' name.

24. Every enemy of my marriage, family, and job, scatter in Jesus' name.

25. Every trespassing power that is harassing my marriage, family, and job, die in Jesus' name.

26. Every fountain of sickness in my body, I cast you out in Jesus' name.

27. Every source of failure in my life, I sentence you to death, in Jesus' name.

28. I command every stronghold of Satan in my body to die, in the name of Jesus.

29. Every killing incantation, backfire, in Jesus' name.

30. Every root of captivity, die in Jesus' name.

31. Personal and spiritual chains break in Jesus' name.

32. Ancestral spiritual chains break, in Jesus' name.

33. Every ancient prison door in my family line, break in Jesus' name.

34. I renounce, reject, and reverse all Satanic plots directed against my life and my family, in Jesus' name.

35. I nullify all Satanic activities, which have been passed on to me by my ancestors in Jesus' name.

36. I rebuke all ancestral iniquities and their effect on my life in Jesus' name.

37. I reject, rebuke, and renounce all blood sacrifices by which Satan might claim me and my family, in Jesus' name.

38. I revoke any curses pronounced against my life and my family in Jesus' name.

39. I shall not die but live and declare the works of the Lord in Jesus' name.

40. I reject and resist the spirit of stagnation in my life in Jesus' name.

41. I bind and cast out the spirit of miscarriage in Jesus' name.

42. I break every spiritual marriage in the name of Jesus.

43. I disconnect myself from every ancestral curse in Jesus' name.

44. I free myself from the spirit of setback in Jesus' name.

45. I release my husband into manifestation in Jesus' name.

46. I release my wife into manifestation in Jesus' name. I release my children into manifestation in Jesus' name.

47. I destroy the activities of false prophets and witches in my family in Jesus' name.

48. I set to naught the evil plans of the enemy in Jesus' name.

49. I command every frustrating spirit in my life to die, in Jesus' name.

50. I nullify every evil covenant working against me in Jesus' name.

51. I clear every Satanic roadblock hindering my progress in Jesus' name.

52. I command every altars raised against me by witches to collapse in Jesus' name.

53. I fire back every arrow of death, sickness, miscarriage, poverty, and doom in Jesus' name.

54. I release the fire of God into the meeting place of my enemies in Jesus name.

55. I set confusion and commotion into the meeting place of my enemies in Jesus' name.

56. I blind every agent of the devil monitoring my life in Jesus' name.

57. I root out every Satanic sickness in my body in Jesus' name.

58. I bind every spirit influencing my spouse's mind in Jesus' name.

59. I come against every spirit of strife, divorce, and misunderstanding in Jesus' name.

60. I command the peace of God in my marriage in Jesus' name.

61. I cover myself with the blood of Jesus, in Jesus' name.

62. Every mark of failure, infirmity, and defeat on my life, be rubbed off with the blood of Jesus.

63. Lord, anywhere my name is called for evil, let fire and thunder fall there, in the name of Jesus.

64. Lord, give me the power to mount up with wings like the eagle, in Jesus' name.

65. Let fire come down and suppress my oppressors, in Jesus' name.

66. Let the God of Elijah divide my Jordan, in Jesus' name.

67. Every Satanic prediction and expectation for my life, I command you to be destroyed, in the name of Jesus.

68. Every stronghold binding me with stagnancy, I command you to be destroyed, in the name of Jesus.

69. Every power of failure, frustration, and backwardness, I command you to be destroyed in the name of Jesus.

70. Every killing, stealing, and destroying spirit, I cast you out from my life, in the name of Jesus.

71. Every Satanic eye monitoring my success and progress, receive blindness, in the name of Jesus.

72. Every power of failure and setback at the edge of success, I cast you out from my life, in the name of Jesus.

73. Every Satanic gathering against my success, scatter by fire, in the name of Jesus.

74. Every mark of failure at the edge of success is wiped off by the blood of Jesus.

CHAPTER 10

Prophetic Declarations

1. **I shall not die but live and declare the works of the Lord.**

2. I shall not be stopped by disappointments and discouragement.

3. **I shall fulfill the purposes of God for my life.**

4. My success is not dependent on luck or chance but on the Lord.

5. **All things are possible with God and I choose to believe in Him.**

6. I shall not drink the water of affliction.

7. **No evil shall befall me; neither shall any plague or calamity come near my dwelling.**

8. I am redeemed from the curse of sickness and I refuse to accept its symptoms.

9. **I shall not be afraid of the future because I trust in the Lord.**

10. I am not moved by what I see, hear, or any circumstances. I am only moved by the word of God.

11. **I dwell in the secret place of the Most High.**

12. The angels of the Lord encamp around me and deliver me from every evil power.

13. **I shall not be afraid, anxious, or depressed by anything because God is in control of my situation.**

14. The Lord is my shield, my glory, and the lifter of my head.

15. **I will not pity myself or allow any body to pity me because my time will surely come in Jesus' name.**

16. I will pay no mind to ignorant people. I will just do the right things.

17. **When I am afraid I will trust in the Lord.**

18. No weapon formed against me shall prosper.

19. **Every lips lifted against me in judgment is already condemned.**

20. I am too blessed of the Lord to be cursed.

21. **If God be for me who can come against me.**

22. I am somebody in the sight of God and that is what counts.

23. **I refuse to be a product of people's opinion; I will follow the lead of Jesus.**

24. My light will shine so bright that it will blind my enemies in Jesus' name.

25. **The best is yet to come so I am cool for now.**

26. I will increase my faith in the Lord and trust Him for every thing.

27. **Whatever has been scattered in my life will be gathered one more time in Jesus' name.**

28. Whatever plot is against me will be brought to an end. Trouble will not come back the second time in Jesus' name.

29. **Whatever they have devised against me will not stand.**

30. Affliction will not rise the second time in Jesus' name.

31. **Whatever they are thinking negatively against me will not come to pass. Their counsel will be brought to nothing. Distress will not visit me the second time in Jesus' name.**

32. Whatever they are imagining against me will be aborted. Their secret conspiracy will not be carried through. My haters will not rise up against me the second time in Jesus' name.

33. **There is no curse against me, no divination against me because I am covered by the blood of Jesus.**

34. No curse can touch me, no magic has power against me because I am sheltered by the blood of Jesus.

35. **There is no sorcery against me, no witchcraft power against me because I am hidden in the secret place of the Most High God.**

36. There is no omen against me, no voodoo power against me because I am a child of God and Jesus is my Savior.

37. **No spell can curse me, no black power can harm me because greater is He who lives in me than any power from Satan.**

38. No evil power has effect against me, no secret art has any power over me because I am surrounded by horses and chariots of fire in Jesus' name.

39. **There is no enchantment against me, no soothsaying and magic against me because the angels of the Lord encamp round about me to deliver me from the snare of the fowler.**

40. He who blesses me will be blessed and he who curses me will be cursed.

41. **All curses turn into blessing when they see the blood of Jesus and the favor of God in my life.**

42. I am blessed and highly favored by God.

Conclusion

The Bible says, **"My people are destroyed for lack of knowledge. Because you have rejected knowledge, I also will reject you from being my priest. Since you have forgotten the law of your God. I also will forget your children."** (Hosea 4:6) **"And ye shall know the truth, and the truth shall make you free."** (John 8:32)

Ignorance is a very bad spiritual disease. Ignorance is no excuse in spiritual matters. The devil seeks to take advantage of our ignorance and rob us off our blessings. Satan keeps on harassing us because we encourage him. Satan's success depends on two major things: **Ignorance and darkness**. Therefore when the light of God's truth is turned on Satan is exposed and his operations are destroyed. **This is all the matter, as Christians, we do not have to accept the negative things the devil throws at us especially now that we are born-again, filled with the Holy Ghost, and know our rights. We have to refuse, reject, renounce, revoke, reverse, and replace the negative things with positive things from the Lord.** We do not have to allow the devil to steal, kill, and destroy what the Lord has blessed us with. We have been given the power to resist the devil and his agents and they will flee from us. I have personally been impacted by the truth in this book and I pray that this book will also have an impact in your life. It is my fervent prayer that the pages of this book will sensitize your spirit. May your spiritual eyes be opened and may you receive power from on high to dispossess the devil and possess your possession in name. It is time to take back from the devil what has been stolen from you.

It is time to gather what has been scattered by the devil. It is high time the witches and wizards in your family know that you are untouchable, unconquerable, unstoppable, and "undonatable" in Jesus' name. May you begin to frustrate, disgrace, and humiliate the works of Satan in Jesus' name. **For some of us, our breakthroughs are long overdue and it is time we called on the God of Elijah to answer us by fire in Jesus' name. Some of us have been waiting for a long time for the Lord Jesus to touch us but it is time we touched him with the touch of faith and draw our breakthrough from Him like the woman with the issue of blood.** The blessings and the breakthroughs are not going to be handed to us on a silver platter. They are to be taken by faith and prayers. **Our spiritual input will determine our physical output.** We must go out and claim the promises of God with holy aggression. **Desperate times call for desperate measures.**

"From the day of John the Baptist until now the kingdom of heaven has suffered violence, and the violent take it by force."(Matthew 11:12)

I see you taking your marriage by force in Jesus' name. I see you taking your children by force in Jesus' name. I see you taking your job by force in Jesus' name and I see you taking your healing by force in the name of Jesus. May the Holy Spirit help you to rightly diagnose the root cause of any problem that you are facing and may He give you wisdom and strength to deal with the problem appropriately. You are more than a conqueror in Jesus' name.

Information about the Prayer Line

Join us on **Tuesdays and Fridays** for prayers on the prayer line. We fast every Tuesdays and Fridays from 6:00 am to 6:00 pm. It is water fasting meaning you drink only water during the fast and eat when you break at 6:00 pm.

Prayer line number: 559-726-1200 and Access#: 950014#

Hours for Prayers:

Tuesdays: 10:00 pm Est, 9:00 pm Cst, 8:00 pm Mst, 7:00 pm Pst.

Fridays: 11:00 pm Est, 10:00 pm Cst, 9:00 pm Mst, 8:00 pm Pst.

Scriptures for the Fasting and Prayers:

Jeremiah 33 vs. 3

Matthew 7 vs. 7

Mark 11 vs. 22 - 24

Ephesians 3 vs. 20

Ezra 8 vs. 21 and 31 -32

Isaiah 58 vs. 6

Isaiah 40 vs. 31

You can listen and join the prayer line on internet radio: www.blogtalkradio.com/kwaku-boachie

You can join the prayer line from outside America through my **skype: Kayboachie**

Facebook: Kay Boachie

Email: ookaku55@yahoo.com

Website for Prayer Line: www.freshfireprayer.com

Contact number: **443-975-5303**

The First week or second week of every month we have a one week fasting and prayers to wait on the Lord. We meet regularly on the prayer line in the evening for prayer.

We have three conferences in a given year. Call and find out about when the next **'HOUR OF POWER WITH JESUS CONFERENCE'** is coming on. Conference is designed to deal with curses and strong-holds talked about in this book. If you need deliverance then make arrangement and join the HOUR OF POWER CONFERENCE.

Sunday Service

We meet every Sunday From 4:00pm to 6:00pm for prayers. We are currently meeting at:

Walker Mill Baptist Church

1948 County Road

District Heights, MD 20747

FINAL PRAYER

YOU CAN OVERCOME Satan TODAY BY THE BLOOD OF JESUS CHRIST.
Satan, I USE THE BLOOD OF JESUS TO OVERCOME, OVERPOWER, OVERTHROW YOU IN JESUS NAME. I SUBDUE YOU AND YOUR DEMONS BY THE BLOOD OF JESUS CHRIST IN JESUS NAME. YOU WILL NOT PREVAIL AGAINST ME AND MY FAMILY. YOUR HOLD OVER MY LIFE AND DESTINY IS BROKEN IN JESUS NAME. YOUR REIGN IN MY LIFE, DESTINY, FAMILY AND MARRIAGE IS OVERTHROWN BY THE BLOOD OF JESUS CHRIST IN JESUS NAME. YOUR OPERATIONS AND WORKS AGAINST ME AND MY FAMILY IS TOTALLY AND COMPLETELY DESTROYED AND TERMINATED IN JESUS NAME.

I RECEIVE MY MIRACLE, BREAKTHROUGH, LIBERTY AND FREEDOM FROM YOUR BONDAGE IN JESUS NAME. I REBUKE AND RESIST YOU AND YOUR DEMONS BY THE BLOOD OF JESUS IN JESUS NAME.
YOU CANNOT TOUCH ME AND MY FAMILY BECAUSE WE ARE COVERED BY THE PRECIOUS BLOOD OF JESUS CHRIST WHICH DEFEATED YOU OVER 2000 YEARS AGO.
Satan YOU ARE A LIAR AND I REFUSE TO PAY ATTENTION TO YOUR LIES.

9 781478 745310